The Redundancy Book

The Redundancy Book

*Transitioning to Success after
Losing Your Job*

KITE BOOKS

Published by Kite Books
an imprint of Blackhall Publishing
Lonsdale House
Avoca Avenue
Blackrock
Co. Dublin
Ireland

e-mail: info@blackhallpublishing.com
www.blackhallpublishing.com

ISBN: 978-1-84218-180-5

A catalogue record for this book is available from the British Library.

Printed in the UK by Athenaeum Press Ltd.

Foreword

When Lehman Brothers in the United States collapsed, the tectonic plates of the global economy shifted. Because of the interconnectedness of the global economy, this had an enormous impact on Ireland. Much of our economic prosperity in recent years was dependent on American investment. Following Wall Street's economic earthquake, that equation changed.

Multinational companies reduced their investments and some closed down operations and shifted their focus to the lower-wage economies of Eastern Europe, Asia and South America. Domestically, the collapse of the building industry and our banking crisis added to the economic woes and led to a downturn in which we've witnessed an enormous spike in unemployment. Redundancy has spared no sector and, this time around, people at every organisational level have been affected. As head of a third-level institution, I've seen these extraordinary developments impact former graduates and our crop of current students – many of whom are regarding the future with some concern.

The Redundancy Book is therefore particularly timely. Tom McGuinness, contributing editor, has welded a range of professional insights and expertise into a clear, concise and useable volume. Perhaps most importantly, this book explodes the myth that in uncertain economic times there are few options. With a practical, positive focus, the book presents a range of possibilities.

From dealing with your former organisation to laying the groundwork for your future success, *The Redundancy Book* offers a practical guide to help you through what is undoubtedly a stressful experience. This book helps you to assess your current financial situation, offers insights into tax benefits and presents tips on designing a fresh, competitive CV. It contains powerful advice around re-skilling to meet the needs of a knowledge-based economy and information on working abroad.

Finally, *The Redundancy Book* charts the path to take if you wish to enter the world of self-employment. By placing the onus squarely on *you* as the key to re-building the future, this book will help to kick-start the next stage of your career.

Dr Paul Mooney
President, National College of Ireland

Preface

I was made redundant before and I know it can be a scary thing. Working with McGuinness Killen Partnership Ltd helping hundreds of people who have been made redundant has taught me that everyone faces different challenges. However, you can take practical steps to overcome these and move on to a new and, in most cases, a better life.

There are a number of ways to approach a book on redundancy. A focus on entitlements and job searching techniques is important but is simply not enough. *The Redundancy Book* addresses your emotional as well as your financial position. It is important to know where you are before you move on. It poses the question: What do you want from a new job? It points towards the myriad of possibilities out there and prompts you to look at your existing skills in a new light. Finding something that you are passionate about is important when charting your future. This may mean returning to education, starting up a new business or seeking work overseas, all of which are addressed in this book.

Being positive, flexible and confident in your abilities will lay the foundation for success. Resilience is needed also and this is where your network of friends and contacts are important. *The Redundancy Book* will help give you the start you need.

Preface

Contents

About the Editor

Tom McGuinness is managing partner of McGuinness Killen Partnership Ltd (MKP), independent consultants, and is a senior associate with Cavendish Management Resources (CMR), an international provider of consultancy and interim managers. He has worked as a consultant, manager and trainer for over 25 years, helping organisations and people to introduce and adapt to change, and advising on the correct ways to handle redundancy, including the legal implications. Having been made redundant at one stage himself, he has helped many people deal successfully with the transition to a new life.

He has qualifications at master's degree level in Industrial Engineering and Organisational Behaviour.

Tom is author of *From Redundancy to Success: Powerful Ways of Forging a New Career after Redundancy* (2004, Blackhall Publishing) and has contributed to many other books and publications on strategy, managing and resolving conflict, redundancy, performance management, and employee relations.

About the Contributors

Terry Devitt is investment director with Harvest Financial Services, one of Ireland's leading independent financial advisory firms. Terry has more than 25 years' experience in investment and finance, having formerly worked as a stockbroker and as an economic analyst with the Government.

Colman Higgins is assistant editor with *Industrial Relations News* (*IRN*) and has been with the journal since 1996, as well as being editorial consultant on *Health and Safety Review*. He holds a BA (Hons) from UCC and an MA in journalism from NUI Galway. From 1990 to 1996 he worked for a variety of business magazines and newspapers. He is currently studying for an M.Phil. by research at the Smurfit Business School in UCD.

Dermot Killen is managing partner of McGuinness Killen Partnership Ltd where he specialises in strategic coaching, management development, graduate management programmes, human resource strategy, and policy and change management.

He is a former director of Smurfit Ireland Ltd and De La Rue Smurfit, and has recently been appointed by the Irish Government to the board of Córas Iompair Éireann.

Dermot is a qualified engineer. He holds an M.Sc. in Organisational Behaviour from TCD and an MA in Business Research from Durham University.

Andrew McCann is the author of *Know Your Rights: A Guide to Your Social and Civic Entitlements* (4th edition, 2009, Blackhall

Publishing). He has a degree in Law from Dublin Institute of Technology and is a graduate of the Marketing Institute of Ireland. He has also completed a diploma in Social Studies and training in the area of community mediation. Since March 2002, Andrew has been the development manager for Fingal Citizens Information Service.

Patrick McGuinness holds a degree in Business Studies from Dublin Institute of Technology, specialising in marketing strategies employed by educational organisations. He has also undertaken postgraduate studies in accountancy and information technology. Patrick has studied both private and public sector approaches to adult education, training and development, and has seen how the various sectors have evolved and grown over the years. He has many years' experience working across a broad range of professional disciplines, including finance, administration, marketing and information technology.

Jane McNicholas (B.Sc., M.Sc., MIAAAC, MEAPA) is a senior consultant with EAP Consultants. She has over 20 years' experience in training and organisational development. Jane provides a range of services on behalf of EAP Consultants (www. eapconsultants.ie), owned and managed by Maura Kilcoyne. EAP Consultants is one of Ireland's leading providers of employee assistance programmes. Additionally, Jane is a psychotherapist with a private practice in Dublin city centre.

Brian O'Kane is the managing director of Oak Tree Press. He is the author of *Starting a Business in Ireland* and *Could You Be Your Own Boss?*, both of which have their own dedicated websites. Brian is also a director and company secretary of SportTracker (www.sporttracker.ie), a company that brings professional sports science technologies to the amateur market, to enhance performance and enjoyment at all levels.

He writes and speaks regularly on small business planning and strategy. He is currently undertaking a Master's in Entrepreneurship by research at Waterford Institute of Technology.

Brian Sheehan has been editor of *Industrial Relations News* (*IRN*) since 1986. *IRN* is highly valued by employment relations professionals for its independence, reliability and insight. Brian is co-author of *Saving the Future: How Social Partnership Shaped Ireland's Economic Success* (2007, Blackhall Publishing); a contributor to *The State of the Unions* (2008, Liffey Press); and has contributed a number of articles to academic journals, including the special commemorative book to mark the University of Limerick-sponsored John Lovett Lecture series (2002).

Introduction: Facing Up to Redundancy

Tom McGuinness

Being made redundant can change your whole life. For a fortunate few, it is welcomed as a means of collecting a pot of money and moving on to pastures new. For the vast majority, however, it is a traumatic, unsettling event and, as with all experiences of this nature, people become uncertain and uncomfortable about the future. For those who have to support families and make mortgage repayments there can easily be a sense of being overwhelmed and not knowing where to turn next.

The news in 2009 is full of emotive language – crunches, crashes, meltdowns and collapses. With this kind of vocabulary our problems can begin to take on a whole new meaning.

Confronting these exaggerated fears head-on can create an overwhelming sense of uncertainty that paralyses us. We become risk averse and potentially rule out beneficial options. We can also develop a victim mentality and go into an 'I am helpless' state of mind, leaving us with less inclination to turn around our lives and make them better.

According to Professor Daniel Gilbert in his book *Stumbling on Happiness* (2006), we tend to become too pre-occupied with negative events. The reason we do this is apparently to minimise their impact when the particular event actually occurs. We can then say, 'It was not as bad as I thought it would be.'

In the current volatile economic environment, the road ahead may not be obvious. But, as with every situation, a path exists. There is no doubt that this will be uphill for many people, but each journey begins with the first step. Thinking positively while deliberating on what to do next is essential to make wise decisions. It can be difficult to do this on your own so getting that extra help is essential.

This book aims to support people facing redundancy through what are, for many, unchartered waters. We look at how to deal initially with losing your job; what your redundancy entitlements are (Chapter 1); sorting out your finances (Chapter 2); what State supports you can hope to avail of (Chapter 3); finding a new career at home or overseas (Chapters 4, 5 and 8); becoming your own boss (Chapter 6); investigating educational opportunities (Chapter 7); dealing with the inevitable stresses and strains (Chapter 9); and moving on to build your work life again.

The contributors all have substantial expertise in and knowledge of their particular fields, and they provide valuable insights that will ensure you overcome the challenges that attach to being made redundant.

Why Are Redundancies Occurring?

With banks collapsing and companies going bust, one wonders where it will all end and who is to blame? However, much of what we see today has happened before. Writing over 230 years ago, Adam Smith prophetically stated in his book *The Wealth of Nations* that the kind of speculation we are so familiar with today is driven by a huge thirst for high profits.

He wrote that 'When the profit of trade happens to be greater than ordinary, overtrading becomes a general error' and is 'always highest in the countries that are going fastest to ruin'. Ireland is a prime example of a country that 'overtraded', as Smith called it, or 'speculated', as it is now termed. The global economic turmoil over the last number of years came from the mentality that unlimited prosperity can be created by the unlimited supply of credit.

Unrestricted and largely unregulated money supply meant that funds became available for almost any venture, in particular in the building industry. Recklessness abounded. Prices rose faster than real values. Costs followed suit, not just in the construction industry but right across the economy. At some stage, like in any situation where there has been overspending and high borrowing, the money must be returned. High prices and oversupply brought down demand. Our competitiveness collapsed. Confidence fell and economic activity began to slow, in some cases grinding to a halt. This became a downward spiral that is impacting on us all. The number of people signing on the live register stands at over 400,000 in August 2009. The unemployment rate has jumped from 4.6 per cent in the middle of 2007 to over 12 per cent.

Developers and speculators played their parts. Bankers soon joined in and the Government supported the 'bubble' with extraordinary tax reliefs. Whether as voters or as consumers, we blissfully supported this cycle from the sidelines. Those who had direct responsibility and failed to carry out their duties should be taken to task, but finding scapegoats will not solve our problems. While some may not have reaped the benefits of the recent boom, everyone will be affected in some way by the downturn.

The Future of Work in Ireland

So is there a future for working in Ireland and what will it be like?

Downturns have happened before. Most people are familiar with the Great Depression of the 1930s in America. But in Ireland we had our own downturns in the 1970s and 1980s and following the dot-com bubble of the early part of this century. This one is more severe, but, like occasions in the past, there will be an end. History also tells us that if we collectively make the right choices now, better times will lie ahead.

Even without the current downturn, industries come and go and new ones emerge to take their place. Like people, organisations have a life cycle. New technologies replace old ones. Unless organisations renew themselves and provide new products or services that their customers want, they go out of business. Computers and automation have revolutionised both the office and the factory. Eastern Europe, India and China are now supplying goods and services at lower prices and with acceptable quality.

Just think of how many brand names that were prominent in the marketplace thirty years ago and are no longer available. Look at how many companies have disappeared from Ireland in recent years. Leaving aside overseas companies such as Gateway, Dell and Donnelly Mirrors, long-established Irish companies such as Jacobs no longer manufacture their products in Ireland. This may seem negative but there are bright sides as well.

Originally, the Irish economy was based on agriculture. With the decline of agriculture, manufacturing employment, most of it coming in from overseas, took up some of the slack. Manufacturing employment is now in decline and growth in service and knowledge-based jobs will be the way of the future. These jobs require different skills and mindsets, thus calling for new educational approaches and increased opportunities for people to be retrained.

Inward investment from abroad will not likely reach the levels of the past. There will be much more emphasis on growing our own jobs. Micro and small business management skills will need to be developed, particularly for those companies with export potential.

As a small country operating in a very large global marketplace, niche markets in which we excel should be our obvious focus. We have a strong base of software companies who are showing the way, especially in the e-learning space, social services platforms, banking software and chip design. Self-reliance that looks outwards will be the way of the future.

Ireland also has a strong reputation for internationally traded services, which is a catchall term for the consultancy companies that sell professional services across a broad and varied range of sectors. These consultancy services range from treasury management to education, smaller and medium-sized enterprise development, and environmental services. The areas where Irish consultants offer particular expertise include digital media, e-business, health services and information technology. Most of the companies in Ireland providing these services are small in size and usually supplement their resources with external experts on a contract basis.

On a more localised level, green product opportunities such as energy-saving devices, water-use reduction techniques, and air pollution and effluent treatment technologies offer enormous potential for development and employment. The Chartered Institute of Personnel and Development states that the future is bright for the job market in the green sector in the UK, where a million jobs will be created, many coming through Government funding of environmental projects. A similar outcome on a pro rata basis can be anticipated for Ireland.

Traditional sectors such as the crafts industry also offer promise. The major sub-sectors within the Irish craft industry are pottery, glass, jewellery, textiles and furniture. Irish craft businesses are characteristically small in scale, innovative and are geographically widespread. The crafts industry is a significant employer nationally, providing viable, sustainable enterprises in all areas, including those isolated rural communities ignored by other manufacturing sectors.

In a downturn, sales become increasingly important and job opportunities for sales people generally grow. Consumption of fast food also increases, creating additional employment. Therefore, while recognising we will have to adapt, we should look forward to capitalising on the new opportunities emerging in the future.

What Is Meant by the Term 'Redundancy'?

'Redundancy' has a particular meaning and it is important to understand what it is and the situations to which it refers. The following circumstances must prevail:

- The employer ceases or intends to cease carrying on the business in which the employee is employed, or ceases or intends to cease carrying out this business at the place where the employee is employed
- The requirements to carry out work of the particular kind in which the person concerned is employed have ceased or diminished or are expected to cease or diminish, either in the business as a whole or where the person is employed.

6

All of the key words used above require explanation and have been defined in law or through case law. Even the terms 'dismissal' and 'resignation' can lead to grey areas and have been tested in the courts on many occasions. Without going into the finer points of the many circumstances and the differing legal interpretations, the fundamentals for redundancy to be lawful are:

- The reason for dismissal is genuine redundancy
- The execution of the redundancy is fair and reasonable
- The selection criteria and the selection process are acceptable and fair.

One thing to bear in mind is that, to be made redundant, your job or part of your job must disappear or be about to disappear. It has no reflection on your skills. Although this will not dull the impact in practical terms, it's an important point to help you to achieve peace of mind. A job is only one aspect of your life. Seeing the redundancy situation from this perspective is a step towards learning to deal with events as they unfold.

Why Is Redundancy Occurring in Your Employment?

To come to terms with your redundancy, it is important that you establish the reasons for it in your particular situation.

- Is it because of changes in the business environment?
- Is it because of policy changes decided locally or at headquarters?
- Is your company trying to reduce costs?
- Is it because of technology?
- Is the product or service being discontinued?

Understanding the 'why' and 'what' will enable you to decide on your next course of action.

- Is the redundancy inevitable?
- Is the redundancy fair?
- Are there alternatives, such as part-time or contract working?
- Should you contest your selection?
- Is it better to accept the reality and move on?

Getting clear information and support from the company and from sources such as this book is essential as soon as the redundancies are announced.

The Management of Redundancy

Dealing with redundancy is an emotional experience – both for those who lose their jobs and for managers laden with the burden of implementing a redundancy programme. It's therefore desirable from the point of view of the employee, as well as the public image of the company, that redundancies are handled sensitively and in ways that allow those most affected to retain their self-confidence.

Companies should first look at alternative arrangements such as reduction in overtime and wages, and the possibilities of short-term working, unpaid leave, job sharing, alternative work, sabbaticals and return to education. These initiatives make good sense for all concerned since they recognise the importance of retaining valuable skills and knowledge, while some provide income for the employee pending the return of better times.

Too often redundancy is handled insensitively. The words often associated with redundancy such as 'cut', 'axe' and 'outplace' convey a harshness and disposability that does nothing for the person losing their job. They can also imply that the individual is the cause of their own redundancy, which only adds to their demoralisation.

While progressive companies support those being made redundant with information and assistance, other employers inform their employees summarily or, even worse, employees hear about it first in the media. Many managers are reluctant to deal with redundancy with tactful clarity. It's an awkward situation, so they can retreat into jargon or euphemism. Such remoteness leaves those affected confused. This is not only unsatisfactory but distressing; the impression given is that some anonymous person has callously consigned you and your contribution to the refuse heap.

Feeling betrayed is natural in these circumstances. If the redundancy process is mishandled then this further exacerbates the situation. Redundancy is difficult enough without it being handled clumsily.

The Period of Notice

When a programme of redundancy is implemented, it is normal procedure for the employer to give a set period of notice. This period is often the most difficult. Morale plummets and it becomes increasingly difficult to keep motivation at even minimum levels. You may become disaffected.

Ultimately, working out your notice without unnecessary dramas and recriminations is probably the best way of getting the most out of a bad situation. Maintaining good relationships with your colleagues and particularly those in managerial positions makes good sense, as you may need their support and assistance later on. For example, you will need references from your immediate manager or from the personnel department when applying for new jobs. They may also be able to direct you towards possible job opportunities.

As you approach the date of your redundancy, assessing your financial situation and knowing your entitlements and what State supports are available to you once you are unemployed will be invaluable (see Chapters 1–3).

Impact of Redundancy on the Individual

Whether redundancies are happening because of increased competition from overseas, a downturn in the economy or the introduction of new technology is of little comfort to those who have to endure the experience of seeing their job, to which they have devoted so much energy, vanish. This is particularly so as a job is often used to describe a person: 'he is a fitter'; 'she is banker'. Our job, in other words, is an important part of our self-image.

Change is seldom, if ever, easy. This applies at all stages of life. Yes, in theory, it is perhaps less difficult for the younger person, but older people have the advantage of experience and, in many cases, have a much wider range of skills. The golden rule is to adopt an optimistic outlook when dealing with the issue of redundancy. This can be easier said than done. Being made redundant need not be the end of the world but can be the beginning of a new phase in your life, as the opportunities and possibilities laid out in Chapters 4–8 demonstrate.

Feeling sorry for yourself and indeed your colleagues is natural. However, the sooner you turn this negative reflection into positive action the better. There are ways to recover and establish yourself on a new and even more exciting career track.

Introduction: Facing Up to Redundancy

Dealing with the Loss

Many who are made redundant testify to it being one of the most distressing experiences of their working lives. The emotional fallout from redundancy can involve:

- Anger
- Guilt
- Self-pity
- Shame
- Chronic indecisiveness
- Lack of self-satisfaction
- Family tension
- Apathy.

Experiencing emotions like these indicates that you may be undergoing a grieving process. An initial reaction to job loss can be similar to that experienced following bereavement. There are good reasons for grieving. Something central to your life is being abruptly removed, leaving you feeling unsure, angry, upset and sometimes even betrayed. Perhaps you have held the same job or worked for the same company for a considerable number of years and feel totally out of touch with current methods of searching for new job opportunities. Most importantly, the effect of redundancy on your self-esteem can leave you with the feeling of your life being out of your control – someone else is pulling the strings and controlling your destiny, and this makes you feel uncomfortable and even scared of what lies ahead.

Apart from the obvious financial pressure that comes with losing your job, redundancy affects your life in a number of ways, all adding to or resulting from your sense of loss.

Personal Satisfaction

Having a role within an organisation can be enormously satisfying. To know that your skills and efforts are required and that you play an important part in a wider picture can be immensely rewarding. The social dimension is often undervalued but is an important part of your career. Redundancy robs us of this. We need to focus on positive projects that give us a sense of meaning, socialisation and achievement.

Effects on the Family

Your family may not fully understand or indeed feel the pressures and concerns you are experiencing and may react in a different way than you expect. They may be looking for answers that you do not yet have. They could be anxious to help but may not know how to do this. These and other tensions can, at the outset, make matters worse, but working through them in a positive way can yield long-term benefits and improved relationships.

Members of your family may have their own fears about the future. Their questions – Will I be able to go to college? What about the school outing? Will we have a holiday this year? – need to be talked through. You should enlist your family's support for any changes that are immediately necessary. Once they understand, they can be an invaluable source of support.

Increasing Stress Levels

When someone is in the midst of redundancy, morale can be at such a low level that it can seem as if circumstances are conspiring against them. 'It never seems to rain but it pours' can represent the mood. Stress levels rise. It is important that we come to terms with and then overcome these feelings so we can move forward positively into the future. Remember, whatever the stressors are, it is how we react to them that dictates the level of stress that we feel. Stress and how to deal with it is covered comprehensively in Chapter 9.

Some key tips to control stress and gradually rebuild your confidence are:

- Release and confide your feelings to someone you trust
- Pace yourself – do not rush into the healing process; take time and the transition will be smoother
- Involve yourself in activities that give a heightened sense of personal satisfaction such as a hobby.

You will not be able to move forward until you have faced up to the way you feel about the situation and have taken control again. The support of your family and friends is crucial at this time, so do not attempt to do all the worrying yourself. Those who care about you will want to help, so let them – even if it is just to listen while you talk out your concerns and feelings. Listening, empathising and offering support to the individual who has suffered redundancy is probably the most important function a family or friends can perform, particularly at the early stages.

Moving On – Goal Setting

It is important to redirect your focus as soon as possible from your current uncertain situation to the more positive aspects of the future. Setting a personal goal is an excellent way of focussing your efforts and emotions as you embark on carving out a new and prosperous future for yourself. Initially, this goal should be practical and short term. It could be related to doing up a CV, assessing your financial position or clarifying your entitlements. Everyone will have different goals. The rules of good goal setting are simple:

- State your goal in clear terms – be specific
- Visualise what is involved in reaching it and what it will feel like to achieve it
- List the steps to achieving it
- If possible, break down larger goals into smaller ones
- Set out your goals in a systematic way – one step at time
- Make sure your first goal is achievable as this will build confidence.

You may be driven by a high degree of anxiety at this stage. However, rushing around frantically will not achieve the best result. It is better to take things at a more realistic pace. This will help you avoid making mistakes and setting off in the wrong direction, wasting valuable time and energy.

FURTHER READING AND INFORMATION

Gilbert, D. (2006), *Stumbling on Happiness*, New York: Vintage books.

Jeffers, S. (1994), *Feel the Fear and Do It Anyway: How to Turn Your Fear and Indecision into Confidence and Action*, UK: Arrow Books.

Introduction: Facing Up to Redundancy

McWilliams, D. (2006), *The Pope's Children: Ireland's New Elite*, Dublin: Gill & Macmillan.

Madden, C. and Slattery L. (eds) (2009), *Sit Tight and Get It Right: How to Beat the Recession Blues in Ireland*, Dublin: Blackhall Publishing.

O'Rourke, P.J. (2007), *On the Wealth of Nations: Books that Shook the World*, UK: Atlantic Books.

Turner, G. (2008), *Credit Crunch: Housing Bubbles, Globalisation and the Worldwide Economic Crisis*, London: Pluto Press.

Wilson, S.B. (2008), *Goal Setting: How to Create an Action Plan and Achieve Your Goals*, US: Amacom.

1

Redundancy – Entitlements and Trends

Brian Sheehan and Colman Higgins

In this chapter, we will examine what your basic redundancy rights and entitlements are, including the taxation implications. We provide some examples of the calculations in relation to entitlements and taxation. The Department of Enterprise, Trade and Employment's website (www.entemp.ie) and the Revenue Commissioners' website (www.revenue.ie) should be consulted in relation to individual calculations.

We then go on to review redundancy trends, particularly where enhanced severance payments have been made – a common feature where companies or organisations are looking to downsize for efficiency reasons. We also examine key issues that have emerged over recent years in relation to redundancy, some of which have been deliberated by the Labour Court.

Statutory Entitlements

When considering your rights, first, look at the legal definition of redundancy and make sure it is consistent with your dismissal. Secondly, examine your contract of employment and any specific provisions contained therein. Thirdly, if there is a company-wide agreement, examine the provisions negotiated and contained in it. While the latter may not be legally enforceable in all circumstances, there will at least be a moral obligation on the employer to comply with them. These three elements will be important. In unionised employments, they will be likely taken up by the union official as bases for negotiating final terms and conditions.

The Redundancy Form (known as Form RP50 – available from www.entemp.ie) combines the forms RP1 (Notice of Redundancy), RP2 (Certificate of Redundancy), RP3 (Rebate Claim) and RP14 (Employee's Application for a Lump Sum from the Social Insurance Fund). This new form provides the basis for any rebate or lump sum claim since 10 April 2005.

Please note that an employee who receives notice after 10 April 2005 will receive his or her notice of redundancy on Form RP50. This form will also be used to record the receipt by the employee of the statutory redundancy amount from the employer and will be used by the employer to claim a rebate from the Social Insurance Fund.

The old forms (RP1, RP2, RP3 and RP14) should not be used in respect of redundancy.

Notice Obligations of Employers

The employer must provide proper notification to the Department of Enterprise, Trade and Employment. If a number of people are being made redundant under the criteria stated below, thirty days' notice must be given to the Minister for Enterprise, Trade and Employment. This applies if:

- Five people are being made redundant when the business employs more than twenty employees and less than fifty
- Ten employees are being let go when the business employs more than fifty and less than one hundred employees
- Ten per cent of employees are being let go when the business employs at least one hundred but less than three hundred employees.

These obligations are imposed on employers by law, which also provides direct safeguards for those who are made redundant.

Contractual Notice

Your employment contract must be examined in order to determine precisely your notice entitlement. If there is no such entitlement stated on the contract, then the employee is entitled by law to certain minimum periods of notice:

- Thirteen weeks to two years entitles you to at least one week's notice
- Two to five years entitles you to two weeks' notice
- Five to ten years entitles you to four weeks' notice
- Ten to fifteen years entitles you to a minimum of six weeks' notice.

Redundancy Payments

The Redundancy Payments Acts 1967–2003 oblige employers to pay redundant employees what is known as 'statutory redundancy entitlement'. This amount is related to the employee's length of service and normal weekly earnings.

The latter comprises the total of gross weekly wage, average regular overtime and payment-in-kind, up to a maximum of €600 per week or €31,200 per year. Statutory entitlements are two weeks' pay for each year of continuous and reckonable employment between the ages of 16 and 66 years. In addition, one bonus week is paid.

The following are covered for statutory entitlements:

- An employee between the ages of 16 and 66 (State Pension age)
- An employee with 104 weeks' (two years') continuous service
- An employee who is insurable for all benefits under the Social Welfare Acts and is normally expected to work for 18 hours or more per week.

Part-time workers with less than 18 hours per week do not have to be fully insurable but must satisfy the rest of the conditions.

Employers who pay the statutory redundancy entitlement and give proper notice of redundancy (at least two weeks) are entitled to a 60 per cent refund from the Social Insurance Fund, into which they make regular payments themselves through PRSI contributions.

What Happens if an Employer Is Unable to Pay a Redundancy Lump Sum?

Employers are obliged to make redundancy payments in accordance with the statutory requirements laid down under the Redundancy Payments Acts. In situations where the employer is unable to pay the employees their entitlements, the Department of Enterprise, Trade and Employment pays the full amount direct to the employees from the Social Insurance Fund. The employee sends in Form RP50. The department usually treats these applications as a priority and later seeks reimbursement from the employer via its Redundancy Recoveries Section.

Claiming because of Layoff or Short-Time

Where an employee is put on layoff or short-time working by his or her employer and claims redundancy from that employer, he or she may do so on Form RP9 (a non-statutory form available from www.entemp.ie).

Reckonable Service

All redundancies notified after 10 April 2005 take into account absences from work only over the last three years of service. Any absences outside of the three-year period, ending on the date of termination of employment, are disregarded. When reckoning or calculating the actual length of your service for redundancy payment purposes, the following periods over the last three years of service only should be taken into account (the absences listed here are called reckonable absences):

- The period you were actually in work
- Any period of absence from work due to holidays
- Any period of absence from work due to illness (see below for non-reckonable periods of illness)
- Any period where you were absent from work by agreement with your employer (typically a career break)

- Any period of basic and additional maternity leave allowed under the legislation
- Any period of basic adoptive, parental or carer's leave
- Any period of lock-out from your employment
- Any period where the continuity of your employment is preserved under the Unfair Dismissals Acts 1977–2005.

However, in making the calculation of the length of your service, the following periods over the last three years will not be taken into account as service (these are called non-reckonable absences):

- Any period over 52 consecutive weeks where you were off work due to an injury at work
- Any period over 26 consecutive weeks where you were off work due to illness
- Any period on strike
- Any period of layoff from work.

You can use this online redundancy calculator (www. redcalc.entemp.ie) to help you to calculate your statutory redundancy entitlement. You should note that the online redundancy calculator does not purport to give a legal entitlement to any statutory redundancy amount. All calculations are subject to the ceiling referred to above, which at 2009 stands at €600 per week.

Pensions

One of the key issues facing someone who is being made redundant is what to do about pension benefits. A departing employee must be provided with specific information by the trustees of the pension scheme, including details of pension rights and options available on leaving service. This information must be provided as soon as is practicable on leaving service and, in any event, no later than two months from that date. Failure to meet these deadlines is an offence under the Pensions Act and the trustees could be prosecuted for non-compliance.

Depending on the employer's flexibility, it may be possible to tailor the severance terms to suit your particular circumstances. For example, if you are eligible, you might prefer a larger sum on termination, whereas someone else might prefer a greater pension on retirement.

What can be done with your pension is governed by legislation. Thanks to the Pensions (Amendment) Act 2002, if you leave service after 1 June 2002, with at least two years' service in your scheme, you will be entitled to preservation of benefits. Furthermore, if you were in the scheme prior to 1991, the value of any pre-1991 pension benefits will also be preserved.

You can't cash the benefits on leaving service but you have several options, all of which 'preserve' your pension until retirement. You can:

- Opt to keep the benefits in your former employer's pension scheme
- Transfer them to another funded occupational pension scheme provided by your new employer
- Transfer them to a Revenue-approved insurance policy or contract, sometimes called a Buy Out Bond.

The Pensions (Amendment) Act 2002 provides the additional option to transfer your benefits to an unfunded (i.e. public sector) scheme of which you are, or are becoming, a member and the trustees of which are willing to accept the transfer to a Personal Retirement Savings Account (PRSA), subject to certain conditions.

Particularly for those who have built up reasonable pension entitlements, it is very important to take independent advice on what the best option is for you.

Right of Redress

There is a considerable body of case law and precedents that qualify and add to the statutory provisions mentioned already. Expert advice from a solicitor or trade union may be necessary.

In the event that you think you have been unfairly selected or you have not received your statutory entitlement, you can submit your complaint to the Employment Appeals Tribunal (EAT). The EAT has the advantage of providing a speedy, fair, inexpensive and relatively informal means for individuals to seek remedies for alleged infringements of their statutory redundancy rights. The EAT also deals with disputes under other labour law areas such as the Minimum Notice and Terms of Employment Acts 1973–2001. These Acts cover the right of workers to a minimum period of notice before dismissal, provided they have been in continuous service with the same employer for at least thirteen weeks and are normally expected to work at least eight hours per week.

The EAT also deals with the Unfair Dismissals Acts 1977–1993 and, where the employer is insolvent, the Protection of Employees (Employers' Insolvency) Acts 1984–2003, which deal with such areas as arrears of pay due to an employee, including holiday and sick pay. Welfare offices and Citizen Information Centres provide advice and information. The information service of the National Employment Rights Authority (NERA) offers useful advice as well and is of course free of charge.

Taxation on Redundancy Payments

Generally speaking, all payments made by employers to employees and directors are regarded as 'pay' for tax purposes. Lump-sum payments on a redundancy or a retirement, however, qualify for special treatment and may be tax exempt or at least may qualify for some relief.
Tax exemption is allowed if:

- It is a statutory redundancy payment
- The employment consisted of foreign service and certain conditions are met – more information on this is available from the Revenue Commissioners.

Lump-sum payments that qualify for some relief are:

- Salary or wages in lieu of notice. However, where the contract of employment provides for a payment of this kind on termination of the contract, such payment is chargeable to tax in the normal way
- Non-statutory redundancy payments, i.e. amount given by your employer that is above that given as a statutory payment.

If your employer gives all or part of the lump sum in some other form, such as a car, the equivalent cash value of the item received is taxable.

The basic exemption and the increased exemption are outlined below. On a redundancy or retirement payment, you are entitled to whichever is the higher in your situation.

Basic Exemption

The basic exemption due is €10,160, plus €765 for each complete year of service with your employer. (This does not include statutory redundancy which is tax free.) Any refund of pension contributions made by you is treated separately and taxed at the 20 per cent rate.

Basic Exemption plus Increased Exemption

An additional €10,000 called the increased exemption is also available in the following circumstances:

- If you haven't received a tax-free lump sum in the last 10 years
- If you have never received a tax-free lump sum and you are not getting a lump sum pension payment.

If you are in an occupational pension scheme, the increased exemption is reduced by any tax-free lump sum you may be entitled to receive from the pension scheme.

Standard Capital Superannuation Benefit (SCSB)

This is an additional relief due that normally benefits those with high earnings and long service. It can be used if the following formula gives an amount greater than either basic exemption or basic exemption plus increased exemption.

The formula for SCSB is as follows: take your average annual earnings over the previous three years, multiply this figure by your number of years' service, divide the answer by fifteen and subtract from the resulting figure the lump sum superannuation payment received.

Example

You were made redundant in 2008 after 20 years' service and received a lump sum of €65,000, which is your first lump sum. You also got a lump sum of €12,000 from your pension scheme. Your pay for the last three years before the date of leaving work was €99,000. The amount of the lump sum that is exempt from tax is the higher result of the following two calculations:

1. The basic exemption is:
   €10,160 + €15,300 [€765 x 20 years] = €25,460
   There is no increased exemption as the pension scheme lump sum of €12,000 is greater than €10,000.
2. The Standard Capital Superannuation Benefit (SCSB) is:
   (€99,000 ÷ 3) x 20 ÷ 15 – €12,000 = €32,000

The taxable amount of your lump sum is therefore €33,000 (€65,000 – €32,000). As this example shows, the SCSB tax relief of €32,000 is a higher amount of tax relief than the basic exemption of €25,460.

Calculation of Tax

A certain amount of your redundancy payment will be tax free, as described above, and the balance will be taxed. This can be taxed as part of the current year's income or at your average rate of tax in the previous three years. This second method is known as top slicing relief, which is claimed at the end of the tax year. It is most useful to people who paid tax mainly at the low rate during those three years, but are now paying tax at the top rate.

Calculating Your Average Rate of Tax

First, find your average rate of tax for the previous three years. Calculate your total reckonable income and your total tax paid for the previous three years. Then divide your total tax paid by your total reckonable income and multiply it by 100 to get your average tax rate.

Example		
Year	**Reckonable Income**	**Tax Paid**
2008	€40,000	€13,000
2007	€38,000	€12,000
2006	€36,000	€11,000
Total	€114,000	€36,000

The average tax rate is: (€36,000 ÷ €114,000) x 100 = 31.6%

Calculating Top Slicing Relief

Top slicing relief relates to the rate at which you pay tax after exemptions mentioned above. It ensures that your lump sum is not taxed at a rate that is higher than the average rate at which you were taxed for the five years prior to redundancy.

If you were made redundant in 2008 and the taxable amount of your lump sum was €20,000, it may be taxed at your highest tax rate of 41 per cent depending on your income for the year. If your average rate of tax for the previous three tax years was 31.6 per cent – see example above – the top slicing relief is as follows:

Tax payable on €20,000 @ 41% = €8,200
Tax payable on €20,000 @ 31.6% = €6,320
Tax payable using top slicing relief will be reduced by €1,880 (€8,200 – €6,320).

Top slicing relief is claimed at the end of the tax year in which you receive the lump sum. So, you will pay the €8,200 when you receive your lump sum and claim the €1,880 back at the end of the tax year.

It is possible to shelter part, or all, of a redundancy lump sum by using it to make additional voluntary contributions to a pension scheme. There are limits on the amount you can put in, but these are reasonably generous. The disadvantage of making extra contributions into the pension scheme is that the money cannot be accessed before retirement. Which method is best depends on the individual's circumstances. If in doubt, it is best to take advice either from a tax adviser or by contacting your local tax office directly.

Trends and Issues in Redundancy

Having dealt with your basic entitlements and taxation, let us now look at recent redundancy trends and issues encountered in an Irish context, some of which were adjudicated by the Labour Court. These trends offer interesting insights in how redundancy is handled in Ireland and how it varies from company to company.

Enhanced redundancy payments, i.e. payments in excess of the basic legal statutory minimum, are commonly paid to employees in many cases where firms are seeking to reduce numbers for efficiency or survival reasons. High-profile cases involving sometimes attractive severance arrangements often dominate media coverage, such as those cases relating to well-known unionised Irish firms like Aer Lingus, or the State-owned ESB. Multinationals like Intel and Hewlett Packard, which are both non-union firms, have also in recent years delivered severance terms that are in line with industry norms. Essentially, additional severance is regarded as 'best practice', although it is important to emphasise that such payments are not obligatory.

As part of its regular half-yearly and annual surveys of redundancy settlements, the weekly specialist magazine *Industrial Relations News (IRN)* noted that there was a significant jump in redundancies in 2008. This was on about the same scale as the increase during the 2000–2002 period, except that this time redundancies increased at a frightening pace into 2009. It is too early to see what precise impact this will have on the level of enhanced redundancy payments, save to say there was some emerging evidence of diminishing payment levels in the early part of 2009. Here we look at how some of the main sectors were trending in 2008 and the start of 2009, as the pace of redundancies gathered momentum.

The 2008 figures for redundancies notified to the Department of Enterprise, Trade and Employment stood at 40,607 – up over 15,000 from the 2007 figure of 25,459 or an increase of 59.5 per cent. Similar percentage increases in redundancies have happened in recent years. Redundancies increased by 48.9 per cent over the year 2000, followed by another increase of 51.9 per cent in 2002. That increase represented a 'step' increase in the level of redundancies, which rose by almost 14,000 per annum over 2000–2002 and stayed close to 25,000 per annum each year since then.

Of course, the difference between then and now is that, then, high job creation absorbed the workers being made redundant. This is not happening now. Also, the current recession is sure to be longer and deeper.

In cases where severance settlements exceeded the statutory minimum in 2008, there was strong anecdotal evidence, most likely due to the doubling of company liquidations (from 273 in 2007 to 575 in 2008), that the proportion of workers being made redundant with a minimum of statutory severance payments was higher than in 2007.

The 2003 increase in statutory severance payments to two weeks' pay per year of service (capped at €600 per week) – 60 per cent of which is paid for by the State – means that many of these workers have a slightly better cushion than they would have had in previous recessions.

Just over half of the 2008 redundancies were in two sectors: building and civil engineering (11,975) and 'other services' (12,350). This may reflect the fact that the construction industry was hit earlier, and so was losing jobs for a longer period of the year than other sectors. (Indeed, the high level of self-employment in construction may mean that even this high figure underestimates the true level of employment lost in the industry.) In 2009, manufacturing (at 9,051 for 2008) may go some way to catching up with construction. The following sectoral overview was provided by *IRN*.

While many of the severance payouts in the building and construction sectors would have been statutory-only payments, there were several enhanced deals among construction contractors. These agreements varied, but tended to amount to about one to two weeks' pay per year of service, on top of the statutory minimum. The construction supply sector was also hit heavily in 2008, but there were a number of enhanced redundancy settlements, clustered around payments based on two to three weeks' pay per year of service, on top of the statutory minimum. At the very high end, a number paid the equivalent of six weeks' pay per year of service, but this formula included the statutory element. Included in this higher ranking of payers were some well-known firms: Roadstone, Heiton Buckley and Brooks.

In the electronics sector, there was a major bombshell with the Dell announcement of 2,000 job losses in Limerick in January 2009. The payout was broadly based on a formula worth six weeks' pay per year of service, but this was inclusive of the statutory minimum and was originally capped at one year's pay. The 'cap' was doubled to two years after the initial announcement was made, following calls for higher severance by a group of 100 employees at the non-union company. Major voluntary redundancy programmes in the electronics sector the previous year (2007) tended to use the standard formula of six weeks' pay for each year of service, with some such as Intel paying the statutory minimum as well. At Motorola, meanwhile, a cap of two years was put on the six-week formula.

Engineering companies tended to pay the equivalent of about four to six weeks' pay per year of service (inclusive of statutory). One of the higher packages offered was at Element Six, which offered six weeks' pay for each year of service, plus the statutory entitlements (with a 'cap' of two and a half years' salary).

In the food and drink sectors, the value of enhanced severance payouts have tended in recent years to vary between four to six weeks' pay for each year of service, inclusive of the statutory elements. But there were some exceptionally high payments, such as at Unilever (eight weeks' pay per year, inclusive of statutory) and Jacob Fruitfield (seven weeks' pay per year, plus statutory, with a cap of €155,000).

Continuing what has been a trend for many years, firms in the pharmaceutical and chemical areas have tended to pay higher severance than most other sectors. Most of them have paid out either six weeks' pay for each year of service, on top of the statutory minimum, or as high as eight weeks' pay (inclusive of statutory minimum). While some of these packages were capped (often at between 2 and 2.5 years' worth of salary), there were usually significant extra lump sums paid out in addition to any minimum imposed by a cap.

In State-owned or former State enterprises such as the ESB (State-owned) and former State-owned Aer Lingus (now in the private sector), the packages have historically been attractive. The ESB's basic voluntary redundancy package involves a lump sum based on one year's salary plus half pay from the age of 48 to 60. At age 60, formal retirement begins, based on service projected to that age.

In early 2009 at former State-owned Aer Lingus about 800 workers signed up for a voluntary redundancy package, some 600 of them on the basis that they would be re-employed soon after on lower pay and conditions. Another 100-plus cabin crew signed up for a more traditional voluntary severance and early retirement deal, with applicants only being accepted in the context of the company being satisfied it could meet savings targets. This includes an early retirement programme for staff aged over 55 years, with a minimum of 5 years' pensionable service. Staff with entitlement to an immediate pension within 12 months will be eligible for a retirement lump sum, based on the greater of three separate applicable options with a maximum amount of 78 weeks, subject to the provision that no employee receive more by way of lump sum than their potential earnings to normal retirement age.

Most enhanced redundancy settlements in the retail and distribution sectors were about five to six weeks' pay per year of service (inclusive of statutory), although the multinational giant Tesco went one week higher and paid seven weeks' pay per year of service (inclusive of statutory) when consolidating warehouse operations in Dublin.

In financial services the most significant deal as the international meltdown was beginning was at AXA Insurance, which paid out six weeks' pay per year of service inclusive of the statutory entitlement, with early retirement options. The six weeks' pay formula has been in line with the average for the sector where voluntary redundancies have been implemented in recent years. Like in other sectors, this sort of average could now be expected to come under pressure.

In 2007, the food and drink sector saw some of the largest packages ever recorded, with the closure of Drogheda Concentrates/Coca Cola, which hit ten weeks' pay per year of service, including statutory. There was a cap of four years' salary. In another drinks company, Bulmers, seven weeks' pay per year of service inclusive of statutory was paid, with a cap of €130,000 or 2.25 times annual salary.

The printing, packaging and publishing sectors continued to suffer. Three Smurfit group plants closed in Dublin, with variations from the standard package of 4.5 weeks' pay per year of service, including statutory. This was relatively low for the sector, with Independent News and

Media paying six weeks' pay per year plus statutory, with a minimum payment of one year's gross earnings plus €10,000 and a cap of €250,000.

Key Labour Court Findings

Not all redundancy situations are clear-cut by any means. A number of cases reported on by *IRN* where disputes arose over redundancy were referred to the Labour Court, which as an independent body arbitrating on disputes has produced some interesting findings.

Of the 30 or so Labour Court recommendations on redundancy during 2008 and into 2009, 19 related to a dispute over the terms of a company redundancy package. Access to a redundancy package was an issue in four cases and redundancy selection criteria also figured in several cases. In just one case, there was an objection to redundancies on principle (Pfizer in Ringaskiddy).

For example, at St Catherine's College (Labour Court Recommendation (LCR) No. 18980), trade unions SIPTU and IMPACT first agreed a deal for five weeks' pay per year of service, including statutory, but then later sought seven weeks' pay (also inclusive of the statutory minimum) when they found a precedent for this higher formula. The Labour Court said the precedent had been for one person in special circumstances, but still increased the terms to six weeks' pay inclusive, as the formula of five weeks was now no longer likely to be accepted by the workers involved.

In another case involving two fixed-term contract workers at Sunday Newspapers in Dublin, the High Court overturned a decision of the Labour Court under the fixed-term contract legislation. The workers had agreed separate and lower severance deals than their permanent counterparts, but the Labour Court said they should be entitled to the same formula as their permanent colleagues (*IRN*, issue 31, 2006).

However, the High Court said that the workers had given their informed consent to the original deals they struck, as there had been 'meaningful discussion and negotiation' as well as 'professional advice of an appropriate character' before those agreements had been signed (High Court 2006/4065Sp – Mr Justice T.C. Smyth; *IRN*, issue 36, 2007).

In another case on severance terms, the Equality Tribunal ordered An Post to pay over €90,000 to a worker for refusing him access to a scheme under which the company set up its former drivers as self-employed contractors, because he was over 60 years of age (see Equality Tribunal decision DEC-E2007-034; *IRN*, issue 32, 2007).

One of the first cases to reach the EAT under the 30-day consultation rule for non-union companies was also decided upon during 2008. It involved Jetwash and the Technical, Engineering and Electrical Union (TEEU), and concerned just four redundancies. The employer failed to initiate consultations within 30 days and not enough information was provided, so the workers were given 4 weeks' remuneration each.

The EAT did not have to decide on whether the employer, who did not recognise unions, was obliged to deal with the union, but decided anyway to express 'its view on the matter'. It said that an employer or company cannot rely solely on its constitutional right not to recognise unions when refusing to deal with a union representative in such situations. However, the EAT stopped short of saying that a company had to deal with a union in such consultations if the workers preferred to be represented by one. Since Jetwash did not set up a special non-union forum to engage in consultation, the question of whether the tribunal would have backed such a non-union consultation mechanism remained unanswered (EAT decision PE2/2006).

As can seen from the sample cases illustrated above, there can be complications around redundancy. If you are in doubt about your situation, it is worthwhile seeking advice. A number of sources of advice are listed below.

FURTHER READING AND INFORMATION

Department of Enterprise Trade and Employment: www. entemp.ie

The Employment Appeals Tribunal (EAT): eat@entemp.ie

Industrial Relations News: www.irn.ie

The Labour Court: www.labourcourt.ie

National Employment Rights Authority (NERA): www. nera.ie

The Pensions Board: www.pensionsboard.ie

Purdy, A. (2006), *Termination of Employment*, Dublin: First Law Limited.

The Revenue Commissioners: www.revenue.ie

2

Assessing and Managing
Your Financial Situation

Terry Devitt

For almost everyone who goes through the experience, the first response to redundancy is a sense of panic about money and all things financial. This is a perfectly natural reaction – after all, you have had a steady income up to now to cover your mortgage, car loan, grocery bills and so on, an income that is set to disappear, at least temporarily. The most important thing to remember at this point is that *all* financial situations, no matter how challenging they may look at first glance, are manageable. Naturally, with a sharp drop in household income, adjustments will have to be made. Some of these will be painful initially, but you will surprise yourself at how easily most of the necessary changes can be assimilated.

Your Personal Balance Sheet

The first thing you need to do is to find out exactly how bad or good things are in terms of your assets (what you own) and your liabilities (what you owe). This exercise is a very useful one and, who knows, may even throw up some pleasant surprises. However, the exercise should measure up in two very important respects:

1. It needs to be *thorough* – don't neglect to include all of your liabilities (overdraft, credit cards, etc.) and all of your assets. It is surprising how often savings policies and unused deposit accounts can be overlooked
2. It needs to be *honest* – most people are inclined to over-estimate the value of their assets, particularly property, and underestimate their liabilities. Try to make any valuations of properties or investments as current as possible – in a falling market, many people are inclined to use last year's value and in a rising market the tendency is to project forward.

The following blank balance sheet or 'net worth statement' can be used as a guide to help you complete this exercise. The purpose of this exercise is to show you where you stand. It may also help you to identify liabilities needing urgent attention (more on that later) and assets that could be liquidated in the event of an emergency.

Analysing Your Spending

Now that you have built a picture of where exactly you are financially, you need to take a close look at your outgoings. Most of us manage our financial lives on the basis that the overdraft or credit card bill has not got out of hand at the end of the month.

If, on the other hand, the overdraft or the credit card or both look a bit stretched, then we need to rein things in, at least temporarily. This generally haphazard approach may

Statement of Net Worth

Assets	Details	Estimated Value €
Home		
Car		
Savings		
Investments (unit funds, shares, etc.)		
Holiday home		
Investment property		
Other (e.g. life savings policies)		
(A) Total assets		

Liabilities	Details	Amount €
Home mortgage		
Car loan		
Other personal loans		
Overdraft		
Holiday home mortgage		
Credit card debts		
Other		
(B) Total liabilities		
Net assets (A – B)		

be functional (at best) while household income levels are stable or rising; it is dysfunctional or even dangerous when income levels have fallen sharply. In these circumstances, it becomes essential to detail all outgoings and to identify where savings can possibly be made. This is an important step towards regaining control of your finances.

The table below should help you make a start on this important exercise. It should be possible to sit down and complete most of this table by looking at your recent bank statements, cheque stubs, credit card statements and utility bills. However, you also need to follow this up by completing a detailed record of all spending, ideally over a full one-month period, although a full record over even one or two weeks will be very valuable. Finally, be careful to include outgoings that crop up less frequently than monthly, such as school fees which may be paid once a term or insurance costs due annually.

Budget Estimator

(A) Monthly Income	€
Your after-tax income	
Partner's after-tax income	
Benefits (social welfare, children's allowances, etc.)	
Investment income	
Other income	
Total income	

(B) Monthly Outgoings	
Mortgage/rent	
Telephones (landline and mobiles)	
Insurance (home, medical, life, etc.)	
ESB/gas/water/refuse	
Food, drink and groceries	
Medicines, toiletries, etc.	
School/education costs	
Leisure and entertainment (inc. holiday, going out, etc.)	
Petrol and motor costs	
Loan/credit card repayments	
Other expenses (e.g. TV, Broadband)	
Total outgoings	
Net income/deficit (A – B)	

Spending Cuts and Budgeting

Having completed your personal balance sheet and analysis of income and spending, the next step – the key step towards regaining control – is to establish a budget. The whole process of putting a budget to work is a challenging one and will be felt by all members of your household. For this reason it is a good idea to involve as many members of your family as possible in identifying spending areas that could be curtailed and in helping to put changes into practice. Family members should also be encouraged to come up with alternatives to current spending choices, which could save money. The following list covers some of the more common areas where savings can be made.

1. The Mortgage

You should contact your mortgage lender as soon as your financial circumstances change. You need to explain your new financial position as fully as possible and explore options such as perhaps agreeing a short-term repayment holiday, moving to an interest-only mortgage for a period or extending the term of your mortgage so that monthly repayments are reduced.

2. Credit Cards

Unsettled amounts on credit cards are likely to be the most expensive debt that you hold. Interest rates are typically 14–18 per cent and if you do not *fully* clear your outstanding balance every month, the effective rate of interest can be far higher than that. For that reason, you should clear any credit card balances as soon as your income circumstances change. Once you have done that, you are strongly advised to get rid of your credit cards immediately. It is simply too easy to spend with credit cards and too easy to run up unmanageable debts.

3. Insurance

Insurance is an area where it always pays to shop around. Talk to a broker in advance of renewal dates or go on to one of the many websites that compare rates from different insurance companies. You should also explore payment options that allow you to cover the cost over an extended period, thus avoiding the financial pressures of having to write a large cheque at a time when money is scarce. It is also worth having a good look at the insurance covers you hold and deciding whether the levels of cover are excessive and whether you are in fact carrying protection you don't really need. For example, it is amazing how many people hold life cover well in excess of what may be required.

While the above are some of the bigger areas of spending that should be looked at, the truth is that, if you are diligent, you will find savings under every single heading on the budget list. Here are some random examples:

- Shop online – this cuts down on impulse purchases and saves on petrol
- DIY – invest in a good manual and start doing those minor repairs around the house yourself
- Prepare your own food – avoid the ready meals and takeaways. Buy the basic ingredients and make your own meals
- Car and driving – use public transport, cycle or walk as much as you can. Shop around for petrol and servicing. Does your family really need a second car?

- Drink – cut down on your alcohol consumption. Also watch out for fizzy drinks, fruit juices and so on, which can be consumed in massive amounts by kids and teenagers; encourage your family to drink more tap water (buy a jug water filter if you are unhappy about purity)
- Mobile phone – try leaving your phone aside for a few days to see how much you really need it. If you have a pay-monthly phone consider switching to a pay-as-you-go phone.

Pensions

With a change in your employment circumstances, an area that may require action is your pension. Pensions, however, can be complex and if you have any uncertainty about the status of your pension or whether action is required or not, you should consult a professional adviser. This section provides a rough guide to the pension circumstances individuals can find themselves in when they are made redundant. However, firstly it is useful to outline the main pension types.

Pension Scheme Types

There are two major categories of pension scheme, as follows:

1. *Occupational pension schemes* are established by employers and usually involve contributions from both the employer and the employee to the pension on a regular basis. In non-contributory schemes, only the employer makes contributions. Occupational pension schemes are in turn divided into two broad sub-categories, *Defined*

Benefit schemes and *Defined Contribution schemes*, and these are described in more detail below

2. *Individual (personal) pension schemes* are schemes set up by the individual and have no direct connection with the employer. Typically, the individual makes regular contributions to a scheme via a retirement annuity contract with a life assurance company. *Personal Retirement Savings Accounts* (PRSAs) are a lower cost variant of the traditional personal pension and were introduced in recent years to encourage a broader take-up of pensions amongst the population.

Let us now take a brief look at some of the pension issues that may arise in the context of redundancy or a change in employment circumstances.

Defined Benefit (DB) Schemes

These schemes promise to pay the employee a pension in retirement, the size of which is usually linked to the salary of the employee when he or she retires. Because a redundant employee does not have a particular pension fund value attaching to them, the issues surrounding these schemes for persons leaving employment early can be complex. As a result, beneficiaries of such schemes should seek professional advice in order to explore their options to their best advantage.

DB schemes have received particular attention in recent years in the context employers' ability to fund the pensions promised to employees. Plenty of examples have arisen over the past decade of companies whose pension schemes were underfunded and who were not in a position to continue to meet the pension promises made to retiring employees.

If you are facing redundancy and your employer operates a DB scheme, you may be offered the option of taking a value from that scheme now into a pension scheme of your own. In deciding whether the value decided on is fair, you need to take a number of factors into account, including the ability of your employer to pay you a pension when your retirement date eventually arrives.

Defined Contribution (DC) Schemes

DC schemes involve contributions being made to a fund on a regular basis and that fund being used to purchase a pension for the employee on retirement. The value of the pension purchased will depend on how well the investment fund performs over the working life of the employee. In a redundancy situation, the employee will have a defined portion of the company's pension fund allocated to him and will usually be given the option of transferring that value into a new pension scheme or into a personal retirement bond with a life assurance company. A personal retirement bond remains invested and becomes available on retirement to help fund the pension benefits of the individual.

Self-Administered Pensions

These also come under the DC banner but, in this case, the employer has no role in the investment policy of the pension fund but instead opts to hand over control to the individual. If you are fortunate enough to have a self-administered pension, you will really have very few decisions to make in the event of redundancy. Since you

47

will already have control over the funds assets, nothing needs to change in the immediate term although, as in the case of all occupational pension schemes, you will no longer be allowed to make contributions (not that you would want to) while you are not employed.

Individual or Personal Pensions

These are schemes set up with no involvement from the employer and, like self-administered pensions, will not be directly affected by a change in the work circumstances of the individual. Again, of course, it makes absolute sense to cease contributions as you will no longer be in receipt of a tax relief for such contributions.

Personal Retirement Savings Accounts (PRSA)

PRSAs can be set up by the employer (occupational PRSAs) or directly by the employee (personal PRSAs). Occupational PRSAs are treated very much like DC schemes in the event of redundancy. Personal PRSAs are treated more like self-administered pension funds and do not require urgent action in the event of redundancy, as they do not have a direct connection with the employer. You will continue to retain full ownership of your PRSA when you leave your employment and you will be able to bring it with you to any new employment you enter into in the future. A significant added benefit if you are a PRSA holder over 50 is that you can withdraw 25 per cent of the value of your PRSA as a tax-free lump sum immediately following redundancy. Clearly, this cash would provide a very welcome financial buffer as you adjust to your new circumstances. The balance of 75 per cent remains invested in the PRSA until you retire.

As the above relatively brief overview suggests, the area of pensions is a complex one and it really cannot be emphasised strongly enough that a consultation with a professional pensions adviser is the best way to explore your pension options in a redundancy or change-of-employment situation.

Looking After Surplus Funds

If you are lucky enough to have savings or to have received a lump sum on leaving work, then you need to do some serious planning in relation to the management of that money. The first thing you should look at is your borrowings. High-interest borrowings, such as credit card debt, should be fully cleared if at all possible. Paying off credit card balances is the equivalent of investing money at an annual return of 14 per cent or higher, significantly better than you will get from most investment funds.

The second thing you need to do is to set aside the sum of money as a 'rainy day fund' (or, as one second-time married lady described it, 'running away money'). This money should be put on deposit at the very best rate available. It should be accessible at reasonably short notice but not too easily accessible. Ideally, these are funds that should be forgotten about until you really need them.

As your lifestyle adjusts to your new income level, there will inevitably be gaps that need to be plugged and occasional necessary expenses that arise, often out of the blue, which need to be covered. You will need some buffer funds available to cover these eventualities. However, you need to be very careful to avoid falling into the trap of using surplus funds to support the continuation of the lifestyle you had while you were still in a full-time job. This will not only deplete your much-needed funds, but will make the later adjustment much more painful.

If, after following all of the above steps, you still have surplus funds available, you need to consider your options as to how to manage those funds. The first point to make is that, as your financial situation is now a more uncertain one, your decisions should be influenced more by a need to protect your capital than by a desire to chase a high return on investment.

Investment

When it comes to investment, the broad options (or major asset classes as they are called) include cash, property, equities (company shares) and bonds. The sections below give an overview of the options available under these headings but you are strongly advised to consult an independent financial adviser as a first step.

Cash

The principal options for cash are bank deposits and insurance company cash funds. The main advantage with insurance company funds is that they generally provide full accessibility with a return somewhat higher than most full-access deposit accounts. However, for investment funds, bank deposit accounts are for most purposes a better option. In choosing a deposit account, the first decision is for how long you are happy to tie up the funds – the longer the deposit term, the higher the interest rate, generally speaking. Some longer term deposit accounts will offer you a competitive rate with some limited access to your funds – combining the best of both worlds to an extent.

There was a time when choosing a deposit account came down to the best rate available. The year 2008, however, taught us that banks can fail and this is an angle that now needs to be considered by depositors. At present, Irish banks are government-guaranteed but this is not the case with foreign-owned banks, which may have a much lower level of cover for depositors in the event of the bank getting into trouble.

Property

At time of writing, property markets are in freefall in most parts of the world, including Ireland, and investing in property does not appear to be a particularly clever idea. However, property prices will not stay weak forever and property is likely to become an attractive investment again over the coming years. It is worth looking at the various ways for investors to gain exposure.

1. Direct Property

One crude but effective way of judging value when you are considering the purchase of a second property is to take the expected net annual rent as a percentage of the purchase cost (this is called the yield) and compare it with the interest rate. If the yield is not a point or two above the interest rate, care is advised. In selecting an investment property, there are a number of questions to ask yourself or the agent:

- How would you or one of your family like to live there?
- What is the access to services (schools, shops, etc.) like?

- Is there good access to public transport?
- Is the quality of the building adequate?
- If it is an apartment, is there a management arrangement in place? (This is very important for long-term upkeep and value retention.)

2. Property Unit Funds

These are unitised funds managed by banks and insurance companies that invest in property. Typically they invest in conventional (offices, shops, etc.) rather than residential property and, for the most part, they do not use debt. Units in these funds can be bought and sold by investors at any time and returns are driven by growth in the property market and by rent increases in the underlying properties.

A warning, however – when property markets are weak, most of these funds retain the right to postpone the selling of units by investors in order to allow the fund managers to sell properties and raise cash. In these circumstances, unit funds can be effectively locked down for a number of months, with investors unable to sell during this time.

3. Syndicated Property Investments

Syndicated property differs from unit funds in two respects: 1. they typically use debt in addition to investor equity; 2. they do not offer access to cash during the life of the investment, the duration of which can be uncertain. While debt can be a very effective tool for enhancing returns when property markets are rising, it can be highly risky when markets are falling. For example, a 30 per cent fall in the property market translates to a fall of around 30 per cent in the value of a unit fund investment. A similar market fall in the case of a syndicated investment with debt of 70 per cent will wipe out the entire value of the investment, since the value of the property will then be equivalent to the debt.

Equities

Equities or company shares are the most widely held and heavily traded of all investment assets worldwide. Again, like property, there are a number of ways private investors can gain exposure to equities, with each way offering different characteristics in terms of risk, liquidity and so on. In addition to investor options described below, there are a large number of more exotic means to get exposure to equities, including contracts for difference, options, warrants and futures. For the most part, these involve increased risk and are best avoided by inexperienced investors.

1. Direct Equities

These days, to buy shares in your own name you need to set up an account with a stockbroker, although many banks also offer a share trading service. One of the core principles of successful equity investment is diversification and a major difficulty with direct equity investment is that, unless you have quite a large fund, sufficient diversification is difficult to achieve. Investors in the major Irish bank shares learned in 2007 and 2008 just how risky individual shares can be when the prices of these shares fell by more than 95 per cent across the board.

2. Unit Funds

A more appropriate way to hold shares for most investors is via one or more unit funds. Typical unit funds hold between 30 and 50 different shares. In addition, it is possible to buy and sell units freely (most funds allow investors to trade on a daily basis). The range of unit funds available to Irish investors within Ireland and overseas is very wide indeed and can offer investors exposure to different global regions or to different sectors or equity types, for example, small companies or companies paying high dividends. Traditionally, unit funds had what is known as a bid-offer spread, which resulted in a difference of up to 5 per cent between the buying and selling prices of units, leading to a high equity cost for investors. Happily such bid-offer spreads are much less common than they used to be and most funds have a single buying and selling price.

3. Exchange Traded Funds (ETFs)

ETFs are a relatively recent arrival on the investment landscape and in many ways offer the best of both worlds in terms of direct equities and unit funds. On the one hand, they are listed on the stock market in their own right, while they can offer the potential for diversification that a unit fund can provide, at a significantly lower cost. A good example of an ETF is the ISEQ 20. This ETF holds the top 20 Irish companies in proportion to their values, so by investing in the ISEQ 20 you are effectively buying a share in the Irish Stock Market. There are literally hundreds of ETFs available worldwide, which allow investors to invest in regions, countries, industrial sectors and even in non-stock market assets such as oil or commodities.

4. Guaranteed Funds

Investors looking to protect their capital but who would also like to get exposure to investment markets can opt for guaranteed funds. These funds, supported by a bank or an insurance company, offer a guarantee against the capital invested so that, at the end of the investment term, the minimum that will be paid back is the original capital invested. In addition, there is a return payable based on the performance of particular stock markets (or in some cases other asset classes) over the term of the investment. While these investments are lower risk, there is a price to be paid for the guarantee. Firstly, you will have no access to your cash during the life of the investment and, secondly, if stock markets perform, you will typically only get a portion of that performance.

So, as you can see, there are a wide range of options but it is necessary to think through what you want. A good tip is get independent advice and to take it.

FURTHER READING AND INFORMATION

Arnold, G. (2004), *The Financial Times Guide to Investing*, UK: FT Publishing.

Hall, A. (2006), *You and Your Money*, London: Hodder Paperbacks.

Lewis, M. (2005), *The Money Diet*, London: Random House.

O'Loughlin, B. and O'Brien, F. (2006), *Fundamentals of Investment*, Dublin: Gill & Macmillan.

The Financial Regulator: www.itsyourmoney.ie

Good general source of financial information:
www.finfacts.ie

Useful source of money-saving tips:
www.managingmymoney.com

Another site for money-saving ideas: www.lovemoney.com

General investment and money website: www.fool.com

3

State Supports

Andrew McCann

Whether you have recently been made redundant, received notice you are being made redundant or just received a cut in your pay or hours of work, you may not even know help is available or where to start to find financial help. The first thing to know is that financial help is nearly always at hand. Even if you have never seen the inside of a social welfare office or know where your nearest social welfare office is, don't panic!

In this chapter I hope to guide you, in non-jargon language, through the maze of social welfare assistance. I will look at how you can get financial help with your mortgage or rent, child costs, with plans to go back to school or college or with plans to set up a business. I will show you how to go about looking for a tax refund, as well as how to get assistance with family medical costs.

So, where do you start, what do you need and where do you go? Let's plan your first steps to get you on the path to receiving a social welfare payment.

Losing Your Job – Where Do You Start?

If you have lost your job, or your days of work have been reduced to three days per week (from five) on a temporary or permanent basis, or you have suffered a substantial loss in employment, you should visit your local social welfare office.

It is important to visit your social welfare office as soon as possible after being made redundant. Claims cannot be backdated, and you will always lose the first three days of your claim. To find your nearest social welfare office, check the website www.citizensinformation.ie, go to the 'Find an Address' tab, and put in your location details. The website will then advise you of your local office and its opening hours and contact details.

In assessing a case, we must determine the person's PRSI contributions. When you work and earn as little as €38.09 per week (Class A) your employer generally pays a contribution for you per week. Therefore people in employment make 52 contributions per year. (It is important to fully examine your P60s and keep them in a safe place all your working life.)

There are a number of key questions we must ask in assessing any case:

- Did you leave your job of your own accord or was it due to conduct? If you left your job of your own accord you may be disqualified from receiving a payment for up to nine weeks. This does not mean you wait nine weeks before visiting your social welfare office
- If you were made redundant, did you receive a redundancy payment and, if so, how much? Payments of €50,000 or less from redundancy may be disregarded by Social Welfare from your jobseeker's (unemployment)

claim if you are not seeking a means-tested payment. Payments above €50,000 will be assessed on a case-by-case basis. In simple terms, if you have worked for the last number of years, you will be looking to claim Jobseeker's Benefit (from your work contributions). All 'benefit' payments are generally based on your PRSI contribution history

- How long (number of years) have you worked prior to losing your job? Social Welfare will look at what contributions you made two years prior to the date of your current claim, i.e. Social Welfare will assess claims in 2009 with reference to contributions in either 2007 and/or 2006

- Was the employer paying your social insurance contributions or was it cash-in-hand? Cash-in-hand payments, i.e. working in the 'black' economy, will only cover you for a means-tested payment unless you thought or believed the work was above board. Even if you were working in the 'black economy' questions will be asked about your earnings. So, though receiving cash-in-hand payments might seem attractive, the downfalls are that if you are injured at work or lose your job you are not covered (from a social welfare perspective)

- How much was your average weekly earnings two years ago? Your average weekly wage two years prior to your claim will determine what weekly social welfare payment you will get now

- Do you have a partner or spouse? Is he or she working? How much is he or she earning? Do you have any children? You may be eligible for a payment for a spouse or partner even if they are working part time

- Have you recently only arrived in or returned to Ireland? You must have, on average (but not exclusively), been living in Ireland for the last two years even if you are an Irish citizen. So even if you worked in Ireland 20 years ago but have now returned from Australia, you may not automatically be entitled to a payment

- What is your age and where do you live (do you live at home with your parents)? People aged 24 or under may have to be assessed on their parents' income if their only option is a means-tested payment (Job-seeker's Allowance) and they do not have paid PRSI (work) contributions. The new assessment (since 30 April 2008 under Budget 2008) takes into account all parental income (including any social welfare payments). From the gross earning, deductions are allowable (which include income tax, pension contributions, rent or mortgage). If there is a second property (from which your parents receive an income), the net income is assessed (after deductions). A disregard of €600 is allowable for a two-parent family, and €470 is allowable for a one-parent family. There is a further allowance of €30 per child under eighteen or over eighteen in full-time education (assuming they are not in receipt of a social welfare payment in their own right). The balance is then assessed at 34 per cent. In addition, in the Supplementary Budget (April) 2009, payment for people under age 20 who are unemployed and do not meet the Jobseeker's Benefit payment eligibility will be a maximum of €100 per week. This same rate will apply to your spouse or partner if he or she is aged under 20 years. If you have a partner and spouse and are claiming for them, and in addition you have a dependent child, you will then receive normal full rates (this is discussed later)

- If your hours have been reduced, is this on a temporary or permanent basis? If your days of work have been reduced to three days or less per week temporarily, you can claim a payment for the remaining number of days you would have normally worked. If your days of work have been reduced permanently to three days or less per week, you can claim for up to three days per week from Social Welfare (in this case the social welfare week is a six-day week). If you have voluntarily reduced your working week, you will not be eligible for a payment
- Were you self-employed or an employee? Self-employed persons (Class S) are not automatically entitled to a payment from their PRSI contributions regardless of how long they have worked, as they pay a different rate from employees (Class A) who are protected by social welfare payments, dependent on how much they earned and how long they worked.

What Do I Need to Get My Claim Started?

When visiting your local social welfare office you will need to fill out a UP1 form (available to download from www.welfare.ie or from your local Citizens Information Centre). It is advisable to fill in the form in advance of your visit. Even if you don't have your P45 or a redundancy certificate (P50), call to your social welfare office as soon as possible. In addition, you will require:

- Birth Certificate, passport or proof of ID (picture ID)
- P45 or a letter from your employer stating you have ceased employment

- If applicable, a letter from your employer stating that your hours have been reduced
- PPS (Personal Public Service) number (formally PRSI number)
- P50 (redundancy certificate) if applicable
- Household utility bill (with your name on it) or a letter from your landlord
- A letter from FÁS stating you have registered with them.

In some cases, your social welfare office may ask you to call back (on an appointed day and time), but be advised that your claim (subject to losing the first three days) will start from your first visit.

Jobseeker's Benefit and Jobseeker's Allowance

Social Welfare will assess your claim for either Jobseeker's Benefit (contribution basis) or Jobseeker's Allowance (means-tested).

The maximum weekly payment for a claimant is €204.30 per week, €135.60 for a qualified adult (spouse or partner) and a maximum of €26.00 per child (up to a maximum age of 22 in full-time education).

To be eligible for either payment, you must be:

- Unemployed
- Aged under 66
- Be capable of working, available for and genuinely seeking full-time work
- Have a substantial loss of employment, i.e. at least three days in a six-day consecutive period (social welfare claims are from Monday to Saturday).

Jobseeker's Benefit claims are assessed purely on your previous contributions from paid employment (employees) in the two- or three-year period prior to your current claim. Therefore, claims in 2009 will be determined by contributions made in either 2007 or 2006. In addition, since January 2009 you will be required to have a total of at least 104 contributions (at least two years' service) prior to making a claim. Also, to receive the maximum payment (€204.30 per week), you will need to have had at least an average weekly wage of €300 or more in the 'relevant' tax year, i.e. two to three years prior to your claim. In such cases, a spouse or partner can earn up to €100 per week from employment without affecting your weekly payment for them. No payment is made for a spouse or partner if their earnings are above €310 per week, and in such cases you will only receive an additional €13 per week per child for any dependent children.

Jobseeker's Allowance claims (means-tested) are assessed purely on your savings and/or your spouse or partner's income. As a single person, you may have at least €20,000 in savings and still receive a payment. As a married couple (couples cohabiting are assessed similarly to married couples), you can have at least €40,000 and still receive a payment (it is assumed money in a joint account is separated 50:50). Income from a spouse or partner is assessed depending on the number of days they work, and only at 60 per cent of their income. This assessed rate is then taken away from the normal full social welfare rate for a family of your size, and the remaining amount is then classed as your weekly social welfare rate.

Self-employed persons are assessed differently. Self-employed people do not have any entitlement to a Jobseeker's Benefit payment and are therefore only eligible to seek a Jobseeker's Allowance payment. Their means (assessable income) is determined on the average of their income in the previous twelve-month period and the next twelve months. The income assessment is the net income after deductions. Applications for self-employed persons may require additional documentation, i.e. audited accounts and so on, and on average take longer to be approved and processed.

When Will I Receive My Money and for How Long Will I Get Paid?

After you have complied with all Social Welfare's requirements, all you can do is wait. The waiting time for claims to be approved has been reduced from twelve weeks to less than a couple of weeks, depending on the thoroughness of your application and whether any more information is required. All claims will of course be backdated to your date of application.

If you do not receive a payment within a couple of weeks, you can visit your local Community Welfare Officer (CWO). He or she is located in your local health centre and only sits on certain days and at certain times. To find out where your local health centre is check www. citizensinformation.ie and click on 'Find an Address'. The CWO can check the system to see the status of your claim and he or she may be able to pay you what is known as Supplementary Welfare Allowance (SWA) while your claim is being processed. Supplementary welfare payments are means tested and are applied for using the SWA-1 form. All income coming into the household will be assessed. You are unlikely to be eligible for SWA if you or your partner works more than 30 hours per week or you are in full-time education. The means test (since June 2007) exemption for

SWA is only €5,000, and any savings thereafter are accounted for as means for assessing a weekly payment rate.

You will not receive a SWA payment *and* jobseeker's payments. Your SWA payment will be granted until your social welfare payment is approved and processed. The normal rules of habitual residence also apply. For further information, check www.communitywelfareservice.ie.

Jobseeker's Benefit payment can be granted for up to a maximum period of twelve months (if you have a total of 260 contributions) or nine months (if you have less than 260 contributions). If after that time you are still unemployed, your claim will be assessed for Jobseeker's Allowance. If you are on a Jobseeker's Allowance payment, you will remain on that payment as long as you meet the means-test criteria, and are actively seeking and available for work. In addition, you should visit your local FÁS office to check availability of possible positions or training opportunities. It is always advisable to keep a list of all jobs applied for as you may be required to provide documentary proof to Social Welfare.

Can I Get Some Help with My Rent or Mortgage?

Help is available with your rent (SWA3 form) or the interest part of the mortgage only (SWA4 form). Help with your rent will be determined by your family size (single or married, with or without children) and subject to the maximum rent thresholds. These thresholds are dependent on the market rates set around the country. In addition, assistance with your rent or the interest part of your mortgage is assessed subject to your income from employment (first €75 per week of earnings is exempt, as well as 25 per cent of the balance of your income from employment), maintenance payments (subject to the amount received) or other social welfare payments over and above the minimum amount set for your family size. In addition, you will have to pay a 'housing element' at €24 per week per adult.

In the Supplementary Budget (April) 2009, the Government imposed new criteria for Rent Supplement. Under these changes, Rent Supplement will be restricted to people who are existing tenants for at least six months or who have been placed on a local authority housing list following a full housing assessment.

Other questions relating to your assessment include:

- Do you have a good reason for not living in or leaving the parental home?
- Do you have the ability to meet repayments, taking into consideration rents and income?
- Have you applied to your local authority for housing?
- Have you refused an offer of local authority housing?
- Is habitual residence applicable (i.e. have you resided in Ireland for two years and do you have a clear link to Ireland)?
- What is the interest proportion of your mortgage? The younger the mortgage, the higher the mortgage interest. This is important as the CWO can assist with the mortgage interest only and not with the principal of the loan.

To apply, you must visit your local CWO and request an application form. If renting, you will require approval from your landlord as well as additional documentation in relation to the ownership of the property. If you are looking for assistance with your mortgage, you will be required to provide written proof from your financial institution showing your monthly mortgage payments, and the proportion of loan and interest.

What Other Financial Help Is Available from the CWO?

The CWO may also be able to assist under the Urgent or Exceptional Needs Payment Scheme for help with 'one-off' bills. This payment scheme is at the discretion of the Community Welfare Officer for one-off bills and is assessed on a case-by-case basis dependent on need. Payments may be made for the following:

- Exceptional heating costs (if you are suffering from ill-health)
- Special diet due to a medical condition
- Bedding or other essential household equipment
- Funeral expenses
- Other unforeseen large expenses
- Food or clothing (e.g. after a fire or flood, or for the elderly)
- Clothing for job interviews.

Can I Get Some Help with Medical Costs and Expenses?

Contrary to some misconceptions, Medical and GP Cards are available to working families and not just if you are unemployed. A Medical Card covers GP visits, prescribed medication and hospital stays, whereas the GP Card only covers GP visit costs. Although the income thresholds are low for families (married couples) at €266.50 per week (Medical Card) and €400 (GP Card), these thresholds can be increased depending on the number of children you have: by €38 per child (Medical Card) and by €57 per child (GP Card). These thresholds increase depending on the number of children you have, their ages and whether or not they receive a college grant.

On the positive side, all expenditure on rent or mortgage is fully taken into account (including mortgage protection and house insurance), as well as a maximum of €50 towards a car loan and travel costs to and from work (this rate will vary if you work unsocial hours). Also, all reasonable child-care costs are considered (this would include payments to crèches, child minders or family members), although be aware that payments to family members may affect other social welfare payments on their behalf. Finally, even if you are outside the income threshold, Medical and GP Cards may be awarded dependent on certain medical conditions. Long-term illness cards (regardless of income) are also available to people who have been diagnosed with certain medical conditions.

If you have been unemployed for twelve months (and are getting a social welfare payment) and return to work, you can look to retain your Medical Card for up to three years (regardless of your income) under the retention scheme. Application forms are available from your local Citizens Information Centre or online from www.hse.ie. Application forms should be sent to your nearest administrative health centre.

We Are a Low-Income Family – Are there Other Payments Available to Us?

Family Income Supplement

Family Income Supplement is a top-up payment for families on low incomes (including single parents). To be eligible, you must work at least 19 hours per week (or 38 hours in a fortnight), have at least 1 dependent child and be under the income threshold (net pay) applicable to your family size. All income is taken into account (including the majority of social welfare payments). The Family Income Supplement is assessed as 60 per cent of the difference between the income threshold (applicable to your family size) and your net income. The minimum payment is at least €20 per week and, once assessed, payments are made for 52 weeks (regardless if you receive a pay increase). The income limit for a family with one child is €500. It is €590 for a family with two children, €685 for one with three children and €800 for one with four children.

Support for One-Parent Families

A single parent (i.e. separated or divorced for three months or more, or parenting alone) can seek the One-Parent Family Payment from the Department of Social and Family Affairs if his or her weekly income from employment is less than €425 per week (minimum weekly payment granted), and you are the main person looking after your child/ren. If your income from employment is €146.50 per week or less, you keep all your One-Parent Family Payment (€204.30 per week and €26.00 per child). Income from employment over and above €146.50 is halved (up to the maximum €425 per week) and assessed against a tapered scale (subject to your income). The One-Parent Family Payment is not available to couples cohabitating regardless if the child or children residing with them are from the current or a past relationship. In addition, people seeking a One-Parent Family Payment are requested to seek maintenance from the father of the child/ren. The maintenance recovery section of the Department of Social and Family Affairs may also seek maintenance (if not already sought). Income from maintenance is taken into account when assessing your weekly payment, although if you are receiving at least €95.23 per week in maintenance you may be able to disregard such income from your assessment if you have to pay rent or mortgage in excess of this threshold. In addition, you can also seek the Family Income Supplement (as discussed earlier) on top of your One-Parent Family Payment (subject to your means). You may also seek an extra half-rate Jobseeker's Benefit payment (as discussed earlier) or an extra half-rate Illness Benefit (which you receive if you are sick from work and have the appropriate contributions) in addition to your One-Parent Family Payment.

What Incentives Are there to Help You Study or Return to Work?

The Back to Education Scheme allows you to keep your existing payment, covers the cost of your course and provides you with additional financial assistance of €500 for books and materials. In addition, you can also retain your secondary benefits, e.g. Rent Allowance, for the academic year. If you received statutory redundancy, you are automatically entitled to apply for this scheme. In the Supplementary Budget (April) 2009, the Minister announced a reduction in eligibility requirements from six months to three months for second-level education, and from twelve months to nine months for third-level education, for people in receipt of certain social welfare payments.

The Back to Work Scheme (which allowed people to return to work and keep their payments over a three-year period – staggered at 75 per cent, 50 per cent and 25 per cent – as well as their additional secondary benefits) was closed to all new applicants in the Supplementary (April) Budget 2009.

The Back to Work Enterprise Allowance Scheme supports you in setting up business through allowing you to keep your social welfare payment and secondary benefits. It was changed in the Supplementary (April) Budget 2009. Under the amendments to the scheme, retention of your social welfare payment is only provided for the first two years (100 per cent in year one and 75 per cent in year two). To avail of the scheme, you must have been in receipt of or eligible for a Jobseeker's Allowance Payment for twelve months or in receipt of certain other social welfare payments, e.g. One-Parent Family Payment, certain disability payments, Carer's Allowance or a Widow(er)'s Non-Contributory Pension. Alternatively, if you qualify for Jobseeker's Benefit (with 104 contributions paid in the last 2 years) or are in receipt of a statutory redundancy payment, you may get immediate access to the new Short-Term Enterprise Allowance Scheme, which will allow you to retain your benefits for a twelve-month period only. For further information, please contact your facilitator at your local social welfare office.

Alternatively, if you have been unemployed for twelve months or more, you may be eligible for additional tax credits (tapered) over a three-year period (known as Revenue Job Assist). These tax credits are applicable at the highest rate of tax. To be eligible you must have received a jobseeker's payment, One-Parent Family Payment, Disability Allowance, Invalidity Pension or Blind Person's Pension. You may also be eligible if you have been in receipt of Illness Benefit for three years or more. The job must be at minimum 30 hours per week and last at least

12 months (other conditions apply). You cannot claim this allowance if you are benefiting from a social welfare employment support programme such as the Back to Work Scheme. The additional tax credits are applicable to the applicant and qualifying children (child in full-time education or with a physical or mental disability). The employer will also gain in a reduction of his or her company's taxable income over the three-year period (as long the employee stays with the company). For further information check www.revenue.ie.

As a Family, Can We Get a Tax Refund or Reduce Our Tax Bill?

If you have lost your job during the year, you may be entitled to a tax refund one month after you have lost your job. To claim a refund you must complete a Form P50 from Revenue (www.revenue.ie). Alternatively, you can wait until the end of the tax year (31 December) and request a P21 (balancing statement) to see if you are due a refund. To speed up your claim, you can register with PAYE Anytime (www.revenue.ie). You will be asked for your PPS number and personal details. You will then be sent a PIN code by post to activate your account. Refunds of payments can be processed directly to your bank account. In addition, you can change or amend your tax credits online immediately. You can also backdate any claims for a maximum of four years, i.e. claims from at least 2005 onwards. The tax system either sees you as single or married (which is different to Social Welfare, which sees cohabiting couples as married), so be aware that, if you are living as a cohabiting couple and are not married, you cannot claim a married allowance or transfer credits (if you are out of work) between partners.

It is also important to know that if you are married it may be advisable to contact the tax office if you lose your job, as you may be able to transfer tax credits to the other working partner, thus reducing their tax bill. It is also important to let Revenue know if you are receiving a social welfare payment, as most social welfare payments are taxable incomes. Of course you should also let Revenue know if you stop receiving a social welfare payment or return to work.

Most of the commonly unclaimed tax credits are as follows:

- Single-income families: as a single-income family, if one of the partners is at home minding the children or a child with a permanent physical or mental disability, or is caring for a person aged 65+ residing with you (or in close proximity), the main earner may be entitled to an additional tax credit known as a Home Carer's Tax Credit. This is an additional €900 per year and is equivalent to an extra €4,500 per tax-free earnings. In addition, the home carer spouse may be able to work part time (up to a maximum of €5,080 per year) and still receive a reduced Home Carer's Tax Credit
- Rent relief: do you know you can gain additional tax credits if you are renting? By simply completing a RENT1 form (even without your landlord's PPS details) you can claim relief on the rent you pay to a private landlord (payment to a parent is excluded). As a single person, this can create savings of €2,000 per year tax free (if you are under age 55) and up to €4,000 for a married couple. These figures are doubled if you are over 55 and/or married
- Single parent tax relief: as a single parent, you may be aware you can receive additional tax credits whilst

parenting alone, but are you aware you can receive additional tax credits if you, as a supporting parent, have your child/ren over to stay? This additional relief is not available to cohabiting couples (even if you are not living with your child). To apply, simply fill in an OP1 form. This is worth a tax-free earning of €9,150 per year

- Dependent relative: are you looking after a dependent relative (aged or infirm) at your own expense? If their income is below €12,745 per year, you may be eligible to an additional tax credit of €80 per year, which relates to a tax-free earning of at least €400 per year. This dependent relative may include your relatives or a spouse's relatives. A DR2 form is required

- Medical expenses: do you know you can look to claim back expenses on your prescriptions, doctor or specialist bills, hospital stays or nursing home fees in relation to a close relative? Prior to 2009, you could claim medical expenses back at the higher tax bracket (41 per cent if you were taxed at that rate). Claims in relation to 2009 can only be claimed at the lower tax bracket (20 per cent) excluding nursing home fees, which will still be claimable at the higher bracket of 41 per cent for 2009 only. From 2010 all medical expenses will be claimable only at the lower bracket. Since 2007 there is no minimum threshold for claims (all medical expenses are claimable). Medical expenses may even include medical equipment and accommodation if health care is only available outside the State or, as a parent, you have to stay with a child overnight (certain medical conditions only). Expenses can also be claimed for dental work (even if such work takes place in another country). Claims for routine work (scaling, extraction, fillings) are not applicable

- Rent a Room Scheme: in difficult financial times, you may want to consider renting out a room in your house. You can receive a maximum of €10,000 per year tax free (€192.31 per week), but if you exceed this amount all income is taxable at 20 per cent. Income from the Rent a Room Scheme must be declared to Revenue. This scheme is not available if you rent a room to a family member.

Other tax relief available includes refuse collection (maximum €80 tax credit per year), union subscriptions (€70 tax credit) and tuition fees (maximum 20 per cent of fees up to €5,000, i.e. a €1,000 tax credit). To claim your tax credits, please contact your local tax office (www.revenue.ie).

What Can I Do if I Am in Financial Debt?

MABS (Money Advice and Budgeting Service) is a national body that provides free, confidential and independent service to people who are in debt or in danger of getting into debt. MABS can be contacted at 1890-283438 (9.00 a.m.–8.00 p.m., Monday–Friday). You can contact your local office (see www.mabs.ie). An information pack is available online or by post and will guide you in developing a budget plan.

So, as you can see, help is always at hand. The above only briefly explains the myriad of social welfare payments available. Sources of further information are listed below.

FURTHER READING AND INFORMATION

McCann, A. (2009), *Know Your Rights: A Guide to Your Social and Civic Entitlements*, Dublin: Blackhall Publishing.

Citizens Information Centre: www.citizensinformation.ie or lo-call 1890 777 121

Website provided by the Citizens Information Board: www.losingyourjob.ie

4

New Careers and Job Opportunities

Tom McGuinness

Changing Career

Do you know what career you would like in the future? Do you want to continue in a job like the one you had before redundancy? Are you ready to do something new? Being prepared to change and adapt will offer you more opportunities to move on after redundancy. So what possibilities are there? This chapter aims to address this question.

Sometimes there seems to be more reasons not to do something than to do it. This does not have to be the way. Now could be the time to make the leap. Being made redundant can be the opportunity to change your thinking and your career. There are countless examples of people who have rediscovered themselves through converting a life interest or hobby into an exciting new career.

Your earning power and job satisfaction before redundancy was the direct result of career decisions you made in the past. No matter what qualifications, if any, you have, you can plan now to go forward and have a rewarding future. It may not happen overnight. But, without a map for the future, the chances of succeeding are slim. You need to develop your own map, based on your requirements.

You can earn good money and you can do it honestly and with integrity once you know exactly what you want from reorganising your career, such as:

- Being able to do the work you love and getting paid for it
- Having more time to spend with your family
- Being able to save enough for retirement
- Having more time for exercise and self-improvement
- Having time to help in your community.

Times may be difficult at present for anyone facing redundancy but there are and will be opportunities out there. Make yourself aware, first of all of what you want from your career and secondly of what careers are out there that offer potential for fulfilment and prosperity.

The Future Trends

It may be helpful at the start to examine the future trends of work and careers in Ireland and internationally.

New forms of employment are emerging, which at least on paper are less demanding or more flexible in terms of working time, or offer more opportunities for self-organisation. This is a positive development. It reflects the willingness and interest of firms to accommodate the preferences and needs of categories of workers – especially women, young people and the elderly – for work arrangements that enable them to reconcile work with their private lives, family responsibilities, study and training needs, personal aspirations and the like. 'Non-standard work' may be considered precarious or at any rate have negative connotations for you. However, on the contrary, non-standard work arrangements can match your preferences and are worth considering.

Another interesting feature of the modern workplace is that a vast number of people follow careers according to a lateral or matrix path (a mixture of sideways and upward moves), rather than climbing the ladder directly. With fewer opportunities for promotion, this is not surprising. It's not uncommon to see people move from a job where they managed a team to one where there is either a smaller team or none at all. In other cases, people move to jobs where they can do new things in order to widen their skill set. This may even be a downward step in terms of seniority, but considering a career in terms of simply progressing 'upwards' may not suit you.

Let us examine some of the trends that are prevalent:

- The number of permanent, pensionable jobs is decreasing. Contracting for fixed periods is increasing, as is part-time employment. Some people have more than one employer – they may be a barman at the weekend, a salesman during the week; they may supply IT services on a retainer basis to more than one company, and so on. It is important, therefore, to keep an open mind. Don't rule out opportunities that may give you a very good standard and quality of life
- Outsourcing of non-core activities by companies and the public sector is growing in areas such as

accounting, payroll and personnel, maintenance, security, catering, cleaning and so on – there may be an opening to set up a business supplying these services

- Multiple-skilling and/or cross-skilling are becoming the norm – the most obvious examples are craftsmen becoming technicians and machine operators becoming process operators. But there are many other examples. What areas can you develop to increase your personal satisfaction and your prospects?

- The level of educational requirement is increasing for more and more jobs. To a greater extent than ever, people are taking courses to enhance their career prospects and the concept of life-long learning is becoming a reality in this ever-changing world. What qualifications would enhance your chances of getting the job that you want?

- Service-sector jobs are rising as a proportion of all jobs, while manufacturing and agricultural jobs are declining. However, there are still many niche opportunities in spin-off activities and products in manufacturing and agriculture. For example, recycling and energy conservation related to manufacturing are growth areas. In terms of agriculture, there is growth in the number of farm shops, in organic foods and ready-to-serve meals

- Working from home, while relatively slow to take off in Ireland, is growing and the speed of growth will increase in the future with the development of new technology and broadband. For example, to run a consultancy or be a journalist or a writer, all you really need is a laptop, broadband, a printer and a telephone – and of course the necessary skills.

Where Will the Career Opportunities of the Future Lie?

The Expert Group on Future Skills Needs (EGFSN) (sponsored by Forfás, the State agency on industrial policy) published a report in June 2009 providing an important indication of those occupations still in demand despite the current downturn. The report mentions the following:

- High-level IT skills shortages are still expected to persist, particularly in the areas of software, IT services, systems integration, electronics, integrated circuit (IC) design, automation and process control
- The growth in opportunities observed for scientific and other technicians combined with difficult-to-fill vacancy data indicates that there continues to be a large volume of activity at technician level and that shortages persist
- Employers in the financial sector are continuing to experience difficulty in sourcing professionals in the areas of accounting (compliance, financial reporting), actuarial science, quantitative finance (risk and financial engineering) and underwriting
- The need for further innovation in the information technology (IT) and pharmaceutical sectors will ensure that the demand for most engineering professionals (electrical, chemical, design and development, quality control and other engineers and technologists) will remain strong, especially as there has been a falloff in intake at third level since 2000, leading to possible future shortages
- There continues to be demand for experienced marketing managers and for sales personnel in highly

technical areas which require specialist knowledge of the sector and/or product (e.g. software development)

- With reference to the expansion and diversity of the Internet, considerable scope exists for part-time and full-time careers. Whether it is developing websites, self-publishing, marketing services and products, e-commerce or providing advice and training, the potential is enormous
- Related to the Internet medium, other channels including newsprint, radio and television, though going through difficult times at present, have opportunities in writing, editing, sub-editing, researching, picture researching and design. Courses in many of these areas are widely available in institutes of technology, universities and private colleges
- The average life expectancy for males in Ireland is now approximately 77 years and for females 82 years, and this is growing. According to the Department of Health and Children, it is expected that the number of people over the age of 65 will increase by about 80 per cent to over 800,000 people between 2005 and 2025. People are not only living longer but there has been an expansion in treatments available for medical conditions. Both factors will give rise to an increasing number of health-related jobs, particularly in care and support roles needing to be filled. The Forfás Expert Group on Future Skills published another report in June 2009 on the health care sector. This report estimated that there would be an annual shortage of over one thousand health care assistants and a similar amount for registered nurses in the foreseeable future
- The number of births in Ireland, according to the Central Statistics Office, has risen over the past ten years

from approximately fifty thousand to seventy thousand per annum. This increase in birth rate, despite current educational cutbacks, will give rise to increased demand for teachers in the medium term as this 'baby boom' moves through the educational system

- Environmental technologies are a major growth area. In many cases driven by State financial supports, energy conservation, renewable and alternative sources, water-use reduction and recycling are just some of the categories that present opportunities for engineers, laboratory analysts and environmental managers. One example is the new Building Energy Rating (BER) Scheme sponsored by Sustainable Energy Ireland, which provides openings for assessors

- Prepared meals, takeaways and home deliveries will continue to grow as people go out less for meals and eat at home. Jobs in these areas can be low paying, however

- If you have qualifications and experience in technical or management areas then opportunities may exist for you to become a consultant working on a freelance basis. For example, many engineers have established their own practices in the construction sector following the recent downturn. The advantage of freelance working is that you can combine a number of elements with consultancy, such as writing, training and journalism, to make up a sustainable and interesting portfolio of services

- Perhaps you have latent talents and always wanted to write that article, short story, a play or even a novel. Getting your story or article to the attention of the right people for publication is the hard part. There are classes in how best to develop your writing and editing skills and many are provided locally to get you kick started. Your local library or bookshop may have these classes advertised. Skill, determination and some luck are required to make a successful career.

Positioning Yourself to Avail of Opportunities

These trends will impact on the nature of career opportunities in the future. To position yourself to avail of these opportunities, the following characteristics will be important:

- Adaptability – change will be ever present
- Being ready to continue education and acquire new skills that lead to specific qualifications
- Having IT and computer skills as they will form part of most jobs
- Self-confidence and self-reliance to pursue your goals
- Commercial awareness and management skills to deal with uncertain situations and customer demands.

How would you rate yourself in relation to the above?

You probably have many of these strengths already. Identify them and build upon them. They are the foundations of your future success. Some other characteristics mentioned above may need development – do your own analysis and plan to address any weaknesses. If necessary, get some advice and coaching as this will help you focus your efforts.

Make sure you make career choices that you want and will enjoy. If you enjoy doing something and have a passion for it, your chances of success multiply.

Moving on in your career is not just a short-term decision; it sets the path for the medium term. Obviously, depending on your circumstances, there may not be much opportunity to be selective. However, it would be foolish not to be aware of the changing environment and risk putting your efforts in the wrong direction.

In planning your move forward, there are questions that you should ask:

- Is the sector I am considering growing or declining?
- What new trends are emerging in terms of technology, new competitors, outsourcing and so on?
- How am I geared to take advantage of these?
- How will these trends fit in with my ambitions, lifestyle and desires for the future?
- Are there mergers and acquisitions taking place and what will be their impact?
- Are there specific jobs or opportunities in the sector that are reasonably secure and becoming more important?
- Are there local opportunities or will I have to move?
- Does the sector provide career development, including training and educational opportunities?
- Are new qualifications emerging that are needed if career progression is to take place?
- Would home-based working be available and would it be desirable or suitable?
- Does my experience and training offer the sector what it is looking for?
- Would it be better to take time out and acquire new qualifications?
- Are there opportunities to provide services to the sector?

Depending on your answers to these questions you will be able to decide, in general terms, the direction you want to take and at least not waste your time going down a cul de sac. There are more supports available now than ever before to help you to take a bold step forward to a new future – these will be explored in later chapters.

In considering what options you should pursue, it is worthwhile assessing your own capabilities and the range of skills that you have already:

Job-Specific Skills

These are the skills that you have acquired at work or in education and may include craft skills, machine operation, driving and so on. Ability to understand and operate quality control systems, undertake stock checks, manage documentation and compile reports are just a few of the skills that can be considered under this heading. If you had a job specification in your former employment, it may help you to list these skills.

Transferable Skills

Transferable skills are those we possess that are useful across a large number, if not all, disciplines. For example, IT skills are beneficial in a wide range of jobs; leadership and linguistic skills could be beneficial in many businesses. Project management, presentation, analytical and problem-solving skills are other examples of transferable skills. You may have experience of coaching and mentoring, some of which you may have derived from your recreational pursuits. Do not forget these when making your assessment. Skills associated with working in a team environment and achieving results are increasingly sought after by employers in today's work environment.

Analysing Your Skills

The table below will help you to analyse your skills under four headings – basic, personal, job specific and transferable.

Skills Analysis

Skill Area	Description	Priority Listing
Basic Skills		
1.		
2.		
3.		
4.		
5.		
6.		
Personal Skills		
1.		
2.		
3.		
4.		
5.		
6.		
Job-Specific Skills		
1.		
2.		
3.		
4.		
5.		
6.		
Transferable Skills		
1.		
2.		
3.		
4.		
5.		
6.		

*This is an example of how such a table can be laid out. When filling out your table, brainstorm initially and then make a priority listing based on your strongest skills and what gives you the most satisfaction.

87

Under some of the headings you may not be able to list six skills while, under others, you may be able to list more. So be flexible as regards the number. Having completed the exercise above and given some thought to how your profile looks, you should discuss it with someone you trust to clarify your own assessment. Bundling together a cluster of skills will help point you to the best way forward.

Progressive companies may assist you by funding aptitude and personality tests, of which you should avail. The better picture you have of yourself, the better decision you can make about where you can focus and direct your efforts when moving on in your career.

The most important requirement is confidence to set your goals and to go after them. Most people will probably be aware of what makes them unhappy with their work but may find it more difficult to say what they are looking for in a career. There are tests on the Internet that may be somewhat helpful. These can either be career or personality tests. For those who are quite uncertain, tests alone will not likely be sufficient and individual coaching may be necessary. There are many providers of these services and, as with all service providers, some are good and others are not so good. So select your advisor carefully.

After redundancy, confidence may be low and there is a natural tendency to focus on your weaknesses rather than looking to your strengths. Now is the time to think about these strengths and use them to move forward.

FURTHER READING AND INFORMATION

Dublin People (2009), 'Beating Redundancy with Autosmart Choice', available at: www.dublinpeople.com/content/view/1774/61/.

New Careers and Job Opportunities

Expert Group on Future Skills Needs (2009), *The Expert Group on Future Skills Needs Statement of Activity 2008*, June, available at: www.skillsireland.com.

Expert Group on Future Skills Needs (2009), *A Quantitative Tool for Workforce Planning in Healthcare: Example Simulations*, June, available at: www.skillsireland.com.

Lanigan, K. (2008), 'Redundancy Can Open the Door to Opportunity', The Institute of Chartered Accountants in Ireland, available at: www.icai.ie.

MacKenzie-Cummins, P. (2009), 'Coping with Redundancy', available at: http://content.monster.ie/12598_en-IE_p1.asp.

Sustainable Energy Ireland: www.sei/ber

Talent Fusion, 'Outplacement Services', available at: www.talentfusion.ie/outplacement.htm.

5

Getting a New Job – Creating an Effective CV, Job Searching and the Job Interview

Tom McGuinness

The Effective CV

A high-quality CV is crucial. Evidence of your suitability for a job you want presented in a clear, attractive and concise way can be a very powerful influence working on your behalf. So time spent carefully preparing your CV is time well spent. Don't be afraid to get assistance with its preparation. Bear in mind that, in the deluge of CVs an employer might receive for a job, one of them belongs to the successful applicant. The prospective employer will form his or her first impression of you from the CV and this is often very quickly – in as little as 30 seconds. Early discarding of CVs may be because they are riddled with typing errors, misspellings, poor grammar and inconsistent layout. So if you want to be seriously considered for the job, making a good impression is essential.

Your CV – General Guidelines

Simply put, a CV is an outline of a person's educational and work history, including achievements and interests. Employers and employment agencies will require a CV as an initial guide to your professional character. Also, if your aim is to start a business and you are looking for finance, a funding agency will likely require your career details.

The following may seem obvious, but are worth mentioning. A CV should be neatly typed, laid out in an organised and consistent fashion; it should be no more than a readable three sheets of A4 quality paper. It should be preceded by a covering letter.

There are four firm guidelines that should be followed for a good CV:

1. Keep it simple
2. Highlight achievements and contributions, not just roles
3. Ensure that what is included is accurate and clear
4. Keep it concise – as short as possible whilst getting the point across. It should be about 800 to 1000 words.

Here are some general tips to make your CV stand out:

1. Present yourself positively in both language and description
2. Highlight accomplishments with tight, clear examples
3. Make sure that the achievements relate to the key requirements of the job and subtly fashion your CV accordingly.

Think of the prospective employer who has needs to be satisfied; try and see it from his or her perspective when preparing your CV. The advertisement is important. Let it be a guide to how you position your application.

Start by finding out what the employer is seeking from the applicant. If you are replying to a specific advertisement, you will find various clues that will guide you to the employer's needs. If you are unsure, try getting in touch with the employer directly for clarification. Even better, have a quiet word with individuals who have experience of working within the company and find out any special characteristics of the job that you need to be aware of. This would be of immense value when preparing a CV and later in an interview situation. Many companies, particularly if they are using recruitment agencies, will send out standard forms on request for you to fill in. Having your CV already completed will enable you to answer the questions posed in these standard forms with ease and confidence.

Things to avoid when creating a CV:

- Use of complicated jargon when simple language will do
- Telling untruths about your skills or achievements
- Copying someone else's CV
- Rambling on about a particular aspect.

What Do You Put into a CV?

The following sections are normally included but should be varied depending on the circumstances.

Summary

At the top of your CV you can put in a summary, perhaps in a text box, that succinctly encapsulates you and why you are the right person for the job. It should be no more than five lines and two sentences. This summary will be the first thing that the person assessing the CVs will see and should encourage and motivate that person to be immediately attracted to you and to read your CV thoroughly. The summary has to be right and hit the spot. Otherwise, it could do more harm than good. If in doubt about this approach, it's better to leave it out.

Personal Details

Next, put your name, address and telephone number so that your contact details can't be missed by the employer. Middle names aren't required. Keep it simple as employers sometimes only glance at a CV. Simplicity attracts attention; complexity puts people off. Don't use initials, as they can be hard for the reader to recall.

Always use your full address and include your full telephone number (including area code). An interested employer may just want to pick up the telephone to talk to you. List your mobile number and your email address if you have one.

Date of Birth

You are not obliged to give your date of birth but it is expected. Use your date of birth rather than using your age. Remember '15 July 1953' looks clearer than '15.07.53' or '15/7/53'.

Nationality

For some jobs, this information is very important. If you are from another country, it is essential that you specify you are able to work here, for example: 'Nigerian (with full Irish work permit)'.

Education

In this section, outline your educational history from school onwards. The longer it has been since you achieved a qualification, the less relevant it will be. School and any advanced education information is usually put in chronological order, with your first school coming at the top of the list and finishing with the most recent.
You should include information on:

- The dates that you attended the school(s) – either just the years or the months and years
- The name and location of the school(s) should be included, although the whole address is not necessary. College details should be provided in the same way
- Examinations passed or, if none were taken, the subjects studied
- Prizes or scholarships attained – this may set you apart from other candidates
- School or college activity, especially with a team work aspect.

Employment

This section gives information on the different jobs that you have done. Research the start and finish dates of all your previous jobs, including part-time, holiday and voluntary jobs, particularly if you haven't had much employment experience. When listing your employment history, begin with the most recent job, list them all and end up with your first employment. This is important because it is likely that your current or most recent job is of most relevance and that it saw you in a role that had more responsibility than your previous positions. Employers will take great interest in this. Before you start to describe each job, think of all your tasks and responsibilities and make a list. Even though it may be obvious that a clerical officer would be capable of typing, it may not be clear to anyone who has not done that job. Highlight any unusual skills and competencies that may impress the employer.

When you have done this, list each job, specifying the main duties and achievements. These should be presented in note or bullet-point form, beginning with a verb, for example, 'word processing', 'typing' and so on. If you were in charge of other people in a job, make sure that you mention this at the beginning of your duties and include any promotions that you received during your time in the job.

If you have had many different jobs, remember that the important fact is who you are now and what skills and experience you have acquired. Jobs from further back may show your breadth of experience, in which case they can be grouped together, for example: 'I have four years' experience of payroll and accounts work with agencies throughout the Dublin area.'

It is not recommended that you include details either about why you left each job or the salary you earned. If the employer wishes to find out these things, they can be discussed at interview.

Certain jobs may require particular attributes or competencies. For example, attention to detail may be important for a job in a laboratory; leadership, organisational or team working skills for a supervisory position; analytical skills for a research position; and interpersonal and communications skills for a position in customer service. As far as possible, mention your skills and competencies – whether they were acquired inside or outside of work – which relate to the position being sought.

You should also list your membership of professional or other bodies, perhaps in a separate section.

Interests

Your interests can help to show that you have a well-rounded personality. Any interest that you have or have had in the past that is out of the ordinary will help you stand out. Activities or achievements that make you stand out might very well give you a subtle edge over the other candidates. If you belong to any clubs or any other non-work related organisations, put them here. Be general about political or religious interests. Overall, you are trying to show the interviewer that you are a firm but not fanatical person with a range of interests and hobbies.

Additional Information

This section can be important if you have time gaps in your CV. For instance, you may have taken time out from paid employment to raise a family or to go travelling.

If you have particular skills outside those already mentioned that are relevant, they too can be mentioned here. These might relate to driving, first aid, computer skills, organising or team leadership. This section might also give you an opportunity to reinforce your particular interest in the job and type of work for which you have applied.

References

You can name at least two people who can be approached to provide a reference for you. Alternatively, you could just state that the names and addresses of referees will be provided at the interview. This is generally satisfactory unless otherwise specified. One reference should be your last employer and this is why it is so important that you get a good one following redundancy. Care in selecting the right referees is important as a weak or poor reference will strongly undermine your chances of being successful at the interview stage.

Make sure that your referees are happy to be contacted by a number of people, especially if you are applying for more than one job. Provide the full address and telephone number of the referees. Inform the referees beforehand in the event that they are likely to be contacted. Testimonials are useful but it is likely that your prospective new employer will want to speak directly to your referees. Therefore, it is important that the referee is available to respond to any request. Otherwise this may delay your appointment or, even worse, put an employer off employing you altogether.

Preparing Your Electronic CV

As stated earlier, more and more CVs are being electronically stored, whether you send it in hard copy or electronically. This poses the question – are there special requirements for CVs as a result? The answer is yes. In today's electronic age, you need either a hard-copy CV that is capable of being easily scanned by a company's software or an electronic CV.

What Format Should You Use?

If you send your CV to Jobs.ie or IrishJobs.ie, your CV will enter the overall database. However, if you send it in paper form, employers will be obliged to have the CV scanned and this relies on the software that the company uses to scan. Sometimes this software is quite limited. To ensure that your CV is capable of being scanned and looks well, here are some general guidelines:

- Do not use colour or have heavy borders – just use plain white paper
- Avoid using columns
- Use 12-point type
- Italics and underlines should be avoided if possible.

Key Words

You must have key words in your CV to bring it to the attention of a recruiter doing an electronic search for candidates. When a recruiter in a company wants a CV for a particular job, they will type in a job title in their own database of CVs. If it is a recruitment agency commissioned by an employer, the recruitment agency's database will be used. Current software provides key words that describe particular aspects of a job; words such as information technology, public relations, design, construction, electrical, welder and so on. Similar to their function in an Internet search, key words are designed to help recruiters narrow the field of possible candidates so they can bring up the CVs that come as close as possible to the requirements of the job they wish to fill. Selecting the right key words for your CV is therefore vital.

One way of identifying what key words you should use is to look at newspapers. See what words are used frequently in advertisements for jobs that are similar to the job you are seeking. If you have a job specification, then the key words used in the specification will guide you.

Job Searching: How Should You Distribute Your CV?

Having suitably compiled your CV for electronic use, you can distribute it in at least two ways: you can send it to CV banks such as Jobs.ie or to specific people listed on the www.Jobs.ie site itself. CV banks are databases or files that store the CVs they receive for later retrieval. Sending your CV to a specific organisation has the best chance of success, as someone will almost certainly view it.

The Covering Letter

With every CV comes a covering letter. In today's world, a covering letter has to get to the point fast. In the past, a hard-copy letter might have extended to two or three paragraphs. However, today's electronic world suggests that one screen length is best; otherwise the individual viewing your letter will have to scroll down. This means that your letter should consist of four or five sentences, depending on their length. There are usually three messages you wish to convey:

1. Why you are making contact:
   'I was referred to you by ...'
   'I read your advertisement in ...'

2. Why your CV should be read:
   'My CV perfectly matches your requirements because ...'
   'My success in selling in the same industry is outlined in my CV ...'
   Basically you should outline why you want the particular job in question, how you're suited for the job and what

particular strengths you have that would add value to the organisation. Use the job specification to guide you.

3. Suggest what the next step should be:
'I will telephone you to arrange a meeting.'
'I would be delighted to attend for interview.'

It is likely that you will need a number of versions tailored to suit the requirements of each employer. Your covering letter will possibly be discarded. Nonetheless, it is still critical to ensure the covering letter enhances your chances as a candidate.

The Follow-Up Letter

Another occasion where it may be appropriate to correspond with the prospective employer is after the interview. This is done when supplying additional information in response to questions that arose during the interview and that would support your case. This will show your enthusiasm. While being careful not to overdo it, your follow-up letter can be longer than your covering letter as it is going to someone you have already met. Make sure you end any follow-up with a request for another meeting.

Confidentiality

Confidentiality is a concern for many people. It is not possible to guarantee absolute confidentiality with CV banks but there are a few useful guidelines to follow to maximise your protection:

• Reputable sites will have a privacy statement, so read it
• Ensure you can remove your CV whenever you want to

- Check who owns or operates the site
- Make sure the site is password protected
- Do not put information on your CV such as your RSI number, or your driving licence or passport number.

You can take more extreme measures but these may require specialist expertise and could be an added cost.

The Selection Process

Preparing for the Interview

If you have been working hard at the job search but have not had any success, frustration can set in. This happens, but when it does you should bring that natural resilience that's within us all to the fore. You may also be worried that it takes longer than you thought to get a response from the applications that you have made. This is not uncommon and it may not be a reflection on you. Organisations can take time to receive and sift through what may be hundreds of applications and to line up busy personnel for interview panels.

Suddenly, one day, a call, letter or email will arrive requesting that you attend for interview. It can be your first-choice company but usually it isn't. Even if it is not your first choice, respond. Relish the opportunity to boost your confidence and to put your interview skills to the test.

For those who have never gone through a selection process or have not done so for a long time, this can feel like a daunting prospect. Being a good interviewee, doing various aptitude and personality tests, and attending an assessment centre can be off-putting. If you are not prepared then there is the risk of not showing yourself in the best possible light. Going through these processes requires certain skills. The good news is that these skills can be learned and, as with all skills, practice makes perfect.

First of all find out what the basis and structure of the interview and selection process is. Will it be competency based? If it is, what competencies are being assessed? How many interviews will there be? Will there be aptitude and various personality tests? Will an assessment centre be part of the process? Who and how many will be involved in the interview?

There is nothing worse than being surprised or being unprepared. Remember, selection is a competitive process. You are out to demonstrate not only that you are suitable for the position but also that you are better than the opposition. Preparation and practice are key to your success.

The Job Interview

The job interview process can vary from company to company. This can be confusing. There may be a whole series of interviews with people asking questions that may, in your mind, not make a lot of sense. Like most things in life, you will meet good and bad interviewers. Just because they are on an interview panel does not always mean they are skilled in the ways of interviewing. Remember that they are human too and knowing that will reduce any fears you may have. Take each interview on its merits. In most cases, first interviews will be directly with a company. In other cases, it will be with a recruitment agency.

Interviews with Recruitment Agencies

The recruitment agency may be interviewing job seekers, either as part of a process of registering you on their database or for a specific position within a particular company. If it is a general interview, the emphasis will be on assessing you and your personality. They want to get a feel for the type of work you like and are capable of doing, and the type of organisation where you would fit in and be successful.

Whether it is for a specific position or not, treat it as a first interview. It is important to build a relationship with the agency, impress upon them your professionalism and that any time they spend putting you forward will be time well spent. Creating that impression with an agency will mean being flexible and demonstrating that you're keen and proactive. They'll then see you as motivated and easier to place. Remember, when being interviewed by a recruitment agency, you may be dependent on them but they are also dependent on you to earn fees from placing candidates with employers. So, in practice, there is a mutual dependency. The more jobs they can match to your skills and experience, the more likely they are to get you a job and earn their fee from the employer.

Established recruitment agencies have a wealth of experience and their advice is very useful. Use that resource. They may be able to advise you on areas that would improve your chances of getting a job and don't be afraid to ask them for feedback on how you performed at the interview.

Interviews with Employers

Preparation

Interviews directly with the employer will generally be more specific and related to the needs of the company. From the employer's perspective, they will be trying to decide whether to progress your application and to establish whether it fits with their requirements. From your perspective, you will be assessing whether you really want to work there. Making the right impression will demand good planning and proper preparation. Begin by finding out about the company, its products and services. Jot down a few points. The main statistics are the size of the company, where it sells its products and to whom. If they have published figures on profit and turnover, take a note of them. Don't dazzle the interviewer; just remember a few easy ones.

Look up the company's website – this is one of the easier ways. Get their catalogues or fliers, if they have any. If they have products in the marketplace, become familiar with them. Try to meet someone who has worked or is working for them. Elicit as much information as possible about the way they do business, what they value in employees and what the people at all levels in the company are like. If you are going to be working in a particular section, find out how many are in the section, what skills are required and the role that section is perceived to play in the success of the company. If you have not received a job profile, contact the company and ask that one be sent to you. It is also useful to identify:

- What the key roles in the job are
- What the objectives of the job are
- Whether there are particular requirements concerning safety, hygiene, accuracy, confidentiality and so on.

This information will help you to orientate your interview answers towards the key requirements of the job and highlight your strong track record in performing roles of a similar nature successfully. Compile the information you've collected and identify how your strengths match with the company's requirements and if you have any likely weaknesses. This will enable you to prepare a strategy for the interview, how to highlight your key characteristics and counter questions dealing with weaknesses. Once these aspects have been covered, it will give your confidence a much-needed boost and ease your anxieties.

The interviewer will have a number of points to cover and clarify:

1. Do you want the job?
2. Have you the basic skills, competencies and qualifications?
3. Will you fit into the organisation or section?
4. How do you compare with other candidates?
5. Will you stay?

The Interview Itself

You'll experience both closed and open questions. Closed questions will be exact and require one answer. Usually this is related to your CV and work experience. You should answer these questions clearly and concisely, so have your facts ready. Open questions are generally used to encourage you to talk about yourself and your ambitions. Questions such as, 'Where do you see yourself in five years' time?' are frequently asked. Longer answers are expected from this sort of question but be careful not to waffle, undersell yourself or contradict what you have on your CV. One of the key aspects all interviewers look for is consistency. Inconsistencies raise doubts in their minds and these tend to reflect negatively on you.

The key to all is to maintain your focus on the job you are seeking. Needless to say, arrive on time for the interview and present a clean and professional appearance. If a secretary or receptionist receives you, make sure you are courteous and friendly. Sometimes the interviewers can ask the receptionist for their impressions. While it usually isn't decisive, it could be a factor in final selection when there is little between the candidates.

The first seconds of the interview are of prime importance. Many argue that decisions are often made at this time. A lot of things happen in a very short space of time:

- Entering the room
- Seeing the interviewers for the first time
- Waiting to be introduced
- Maintaining eye contact
- Giving each member of the interview team a firm handshake, if appropriate, and a warm smile
- Sitting down when asked
- Getting yourself seated as comfortably as possible
- Trying not to lean too far forward or back and keeping your hands resting in your lap.

Rehearsing this phase and keeping in mind a positive picture of what it will be like will help you. Listen carefully to the questions. Check understanding if necessary and answer clearly. This will help you make the right impression. Try to maintain eye contact with the interviewers when giving answers.

You are going to be nervous so try to channel some of those nerves into enthusiasm. A gentle smile as you wait can help put you at ease. When people are nervous, they tend to speak faster than normal, so you should slow down your speech a little. At the end of the meeting, you will be asked if you have any questions. Have at least two or three prepared. These should be sensible, the last one being about when you are likely to hear the outcome of the interview. Inquire about the working environment or the strategic direction the company is taking. Don't inquire about holidays or perks at this stage.

Some sample questions at the end of the interview are:

- What is the organisational structure?
- Where does the position fit into the company?
- Is there a performance appraisal system?
- Are there training and development opportunities?
- Are there any planned changes in products or services?

Subtly express how your interest in the job has deepened, how it appeals to you and how you know you can achieve success in it. If you have specific suggestions about how you can contribute over and above the ordinary, state them as you go along or at this stage. If your suggestions are innovative and strong, then this will impress the interviewers.

At the end shake hands and thank each individual before you leave.

Interviewers are human; they will have biases and prejudices – we all do. This may be unfair but, unfortunately, it's a fact of life. If they like you, they will be more likely to rate you better. Being friendly, courteous and professional will therefore ease your way in that regard. Give each question as much respect as you can.

They will likely have a scoring sheet with criteria under which they will rate you. Sometimes this is disclosed and other times it is not. If you can find out before the interview what the criteria are, then this is helpful.

If possible, get some practice at being interviewed. You only have a relatively short time to make an impression and it is important that you use this time well. No one would go on stage or play an important game without some practice beforehand. Rehearsing with a friend or family member could make the difference. List out the questions you might be asked and practise answering them, particularly those that may concern your weaknesses. You can also use a professional coach to guide you but obviously this will be at extra expense unless it is paid for by your former company.

Competency-Based Interviews

An increasing number of employers are using competency-based interviewing techniques. If you apply for a job and are told that the interviewer will use this technique, then it is important to understand what a competency-based interview is and how you should prepare for it.

Firstly, it helps to understand a little about this technique and why employers use it. In a traditional interview, the interviewer will ask you questions designed to let you show that you have the skills and knowledge needed to do the job. However, it is also important that you fit in with the team, and with the employer's culture and style. A competency-based interview is designed to ask you additional questions about your character, soft skills and personal attributes that let both you and the employer determine whether you fit their needs. These are called 'behavioural competencies'.

A competency-based interview will allot about half the interview to your job skills and about half to your behavioural competencies. The interviewer will assess these by looking for evidence of how you have acted in real situations in the past. Here are some steps to help you to prepare for the interview and advice to keep in mind when you are actually at the interview.

Before the Competency-Based Interview:

1. List out all your attributes and characteristics that you think will be important both to you and to a future employer. For example, are you good at handling detail or are you good at looking at the big picture? Do you excel at creative problem-solving or do you develop and follow careful procedures? Are you a logical thinker or are you intuitive?
2. For each attribute, think about a couple of real situations in your current or recent jobs which demonstrate how you have used this attribute. The interviewer will want real evidence that you have this attribute, so having some examples prepared before you get to the interview will show that you have thought ahead. Practical examples and 'stories' of real events are powerful ways to convince your prospective employer of your abilities and motivations. Again, make sure not to be too long-winded as this may illustrate a 'competency' you do not want to show!

At the interview itself:

1. Be honest about your attributes. If you convince an employer that you are strong on precise detail because that's what they are looking for, when really you are a big-picture person, you will soon be caught out once you've started the job
2. Take time to think before you give your example of how you have put a particular attribute into practice. Don't

just rush in with one of your prepared situations if it doesn't show that you have what they're looking for. Ask yourself whether this is the best example you can think of to illustrate the attribute they are interested in

3. Be willing to ask the interviewer to clarify. If they ask you a vague or ambiguous question, rather than asking them, 'What do you mean?', you could say, 'Do you mean such-and-such?' to show that you have tried to interpret what they have said

4. If you have not done a competency-based interview before, you may need some coaching and practice, but if your illustrations are good then it is no more difficult than any other approach.

Psychological Testing

More and more companies are using some form of testing as part of the selection process. There are two main kinds of psychometric tests. Skills tests measure how well you do something, and can be split into ability and aptitude tests. Personality tests measure less quantifiable characteristics – they reveal your motivation, attitude and work style.

Psychometric tests are put together very carefully by experts to make sure that each one accurately measures what it should. They are backed up by evidence and data that shows how well they work.

Most tests involve multiple-choice answers and provide a numerical score. A higher score is not always 'better' – tests often measure multiple skills. In skills tests, the results compare your ability levels to those of other people; personality tests reveal how much of a certain characteristic you possess. These results can be compared to the standards desired by the company.

Ability Tests

Ability tests measure either general or particular types of intelligence. These include numerical intelligence, verbal and logical reasoning, problem-solving skills and the ability to identify mistakes accurately. Ability tests are often confused with aptitude tests, which is hardly surprising since they're quite similar and many tests measure both. Ability tests measure general skills, which you're likely to already possess.

Aptitude Tests

Aptitude tests are more specific. They assess your ability to use specific job-related skills, and predict future performance. They examine your potential to learn to do a new task rather than testing the skills you already have. With the continual development of new technologies, the ability to adapt to change is increasingly important to employers. Those who can apply their experience and develop new skills quickly are very valuable and highly sought after.

Personality Tests

Personality tests assess your typical behaviour and preferred way of going about things. Employers may look for people with certain characteristics for particular jobs. For a sales role, for example, they may want someone who is very sociable, organised and creative. A personality test enables employers to see whether you match their ideal profile.

Assessment Centres

Assessment centres are a process not a place. They are undertaken usually in addition to the interview and psychometric tests, and have grown in popularity over recent years, though – in one form or another – they have been around since the Second World War.

Interviews aren't all that reliable – they have between one chance in four and one in three of selecting the right candidate. This may be some consolation if you have been unsuccessful at an interview as it is possible that the company made the wrong choice. For an employer, tests increase reliability by 10 to 15 per cent. Assessment centres are claimed to increase this further – some claim up to 70 per cent reliability. However, selecting the 'wrong' candidate is a major issue and is potentially very costly. So in an effort to improve the chances of selecting the right candidate, assessment centres try to simulate the real work situation that you will be faced with in your new job and see how you manage or cope. In other words, they look at the future whereas interviews primarily focus on the past.

So what can you expect if you are asked to participate in an assessment centre? Normally, you will be with a group of other candidates for a series of tests or assessments. These tests are designed to show the employer if you have most of the skills you need to do the job well. Each assessment centre will have a different set of tests depending on the requirements of the job. Examples of some of the tests you could face are:

- Technical skills, such as typing, answering the phone, IT and so on
- Logical thinking

- Decision making
- Analytical ability
- Leadership
- Response under pressure
- Interpersonal skills
- Planning
- Dealing with complaints
- Ability to work as part of a team
- Negotiating
- Selling
- Self-confidence.

The exercises that you will be asked to do may be group- or individual-based. Group exercises usually involve being required to discuss a topic or solve a problem. They are designed to see how you perform in a group and focus on interpersonal skills such as assertiveness, leadership, organising or planning. Individual exercises focus more on your personal abilities and skills. These can include composing an essay, reviewing and making comments on a case study, repairing a device, dealing with an 'angry customer' on the telephone or solving a problem.

Case studies are often used and sometimes can cause difficulties. The case studies are designed to assess your abilities to diagnose and analyse an issue, to come up with potential solutions (there is seldom one right solution) and to work generally as part of the team.

A few pointers for handling case studies are:

- Read it carefully
- Note the key points or messages
- Answer the question you are asked
- Keep to the time limit

- Explain the logic behind your thinking
- Make a decision – it is better than appearing indecisive.

In summary, the keys to success in the selection process are preparation and practice. No one does the perfect interview! Some of the tests and assessment centre activities can be a bit daunting at first. So don't be despondent if you are not satisfied with your performance on the first occasion. Keep at it and you will be surprised how confident and good you will become. Make sure to let your positivity shine through and eventually you will succeed.

FURTHER READING AND INFORMATION

Carter, P. (2005), *Boost Your Interview Test Performance: Increase Your Chances of Climbing the Corporate Ladder*, UK: Bertrams.

Rogers, P. (2008), *The Straightforward CV*, UK: Straightforward Publishing.

Straw, A. and Shapiro, M. (2002), *Succeeding at Interviews in a Week*, UK: Hodder & Stoughton.

Taylor, I. (2007), *A Practical Guide to Assessment Centres and Selection Processes*, UK: Kogan Page.

Yate, M. (2003), *The Ultimate CV Book: Write that Perfect CV and Get that Job*, UK: Kogan Page.

Irishjobs.ie: www.irishjobs.ie

Jobs.ie: www.jobs.ie

Publicjobs.ie: www.publicjobs.ie

RecruitIreland.ie: www.recruitireland.ie

6

Setting Up Your Own Business

Brian O'Kane

If you have just been made redundant, or you fear that you might be made redundant soon, you may be thinking of starting a business as an alternative to looking for another job.

The *Global Entrepreneurship Monitor Report for Ireland 2007* suggested that one in twelve Irish people were involved in actively planning or had recently started a business; among 25- to 34-year-olds, this figure increased to one in nine. So you're not alone!

Many entrepreneurs find immense personal satisfaction in running their own businesses, being their own boss, choosing what they do and how and when they do it – and being able to earn a living doing so. A small few make well-publicised fortunes; most get their rewards from the intangibles of self-employment.

Look before You Leap

The first thing that you need to know is that the most critical factor in determining whether a start-up succeeds or not is the entrepreneur him/herself – this is *you*.

Your vision, your ambition, your perseverance, your willingness to work hard and long hours, your commitment, your financial resources, your skills and experience – all these are potential pluses. Against these can be set perhaps (depending on your circumstances) your inexperience in business, your lack of knowledge of the market, your personal circumstances, which may restrict the time you can spend on the business, your lack of the necessary finance – all of these are potential drawbacks. The trick is to make sure that the pluses outweigh the minuses.

Being self-employed demands a lot of commitment. It is both physically and mentally demanding. Therefore, it is very important to ask yourself why you want to become self-employed. It may take some soul-searching but answering this question is vital to your decision to go ahead, since simply being prepared to make the commitment does not necessarily mean that entrepreneurship is right for you.

You need to answer these questions:

- Will you be able to give the business the time and attention it needs?
- Will your health stand up to long hours and hard work?
- Will you be able to cope with the pressures and stress?

You also need to see whether you have some of the following traits, since research has shown that entrepreneurs have:

- A strong need for control and independence
- Drive and energy
- Self-confidence
- A view of money as a measure of performance

- A tolerance for ambiguity and uncertainty
- A sense of social responsibility.

Research has also shown that they are good at:

- Problem-solving
- Setting (and achieving) goals and targets
- Calculated risk-taking
- Committing themselves for the long term
- Dealing with failure
- Using feedback
- Taking the initiative
- Seeking personal responsibility
- Tapping and using resources
- Competing against self-imposed standards.

How do you measure against these criteria? Be honest with yourself.

Next, as you will need all the support you can get when starting up, it is important from the very beginning to involve your spouse or partner and your family in the decision to start a business. Ask them these questions (and listen carefully to their answers):

- Will they commit to the business?
- Are they prepared to accept that you will be working long hours, and coming home tired and stressed out?

Make sure that they can give you the support you need.

Setting up a business has financial consequences that go beyond the initial investment required to get started. You have to consider whether you can cope with reduced and/or irregular income, as well as financial insecurity.

How will this affect you and your family? This is a very important issue because money, or lack of it, can have a huge impact on your relationships, your self-esteem and your stress levels. Think about your mortgage or rent payments, education for your children, social life, clothing, holidays, luxuries and other such factors.

Your views may be coloured by whether you see an opportunity or whether you feel that redundancy leaves you no choice except self-employment. If you are excited about an opportunity that you have spotted, it's hard to be objective and to listen to well-meaning advice that urges you to be cautious, but it's more sensible to tread a little carefully on a new path, even if it chafes. On the other hand, if you feel you're being pushed into self-employment and are not comfortable with it, then it's unsurprising that you see negatives all around. In both cases, you need to identify and isolate your own feelings, so that you can consider self-employment without bias. Talking out your idea for self-employment with someone who can offer you constructive criticism can help you look at it more objectively and is always a useful exercise.

Running your own business requires a broad range of skills and experience. You should assess yourself to see which skills you have already and which skills you need to develop. When you think for a few moments, you will be amazed at how many skills, both formal – how to speak French, how to use a wood lathe or how to use a computer spreadsheet – and informal – how to deal with difficult people who are always finding fault without losing your temper, or how to get people to do what you want them to do when you cannot give them direct orders or instructions – you have and how many may be transferable to business generally.

Look at your education and your experience – not just experience at work but also hobbies, community activities, your family situation and so on. Can this experience be transferred to your business idea?

You do not have to be Superman or Superwoman to be an entrepreneur. All you need is a good understanding of your capabilities and the willingness to fill in the gaps, either by additional training for yourself or by hiring other people to do the necessary work. Refer to your assessment of capabilities earlier.

Last, you need to ask yourself one more important question, the answer to which will have a major influence on the kind of business that you set up and on how happy and fulfilled – or otherwise – you will be as you progress your idea to reality and beyond: What does success mean to you?

Success is not always measured in material terms: being free to work on projects that interest you, with people you like and at times that suit you may be more valuable than 10 per cent, 20 per cent or even 100 per cent more income. Only you can decide what success means to you. There's no 'right' answer, but it is helpful to give the question some thought as you consider self-employment.

Finding an Idea

For most people – especially those who have not previously given a lot of thought to the notion of self-employment – deciding what kind of business it will be or what it will sell or make is the hardest thing about starting a business.

Basically, there are three ways of coming up with an idea for a business: copy, create or find a growing sector.

Look around you. There are millions of businesses out there already – more than 200,000 in Ireland alone. Some of them may be open to replication or, with adaptation, may give you an idea for a new business.

Go back to your skills and experience. Where could they be used? In particular, where could they be used to save other people money (since that's the one thing that everyone becomes very conscious of in a downturn)?

Alternatively, look at bigger businesses – which often miss out on the personal element that is so important for good customer and business relationships – and see whether you could start a similar business, on a smaller scale perhaps but with that human touch?

Could you do outsourced work that you used to do from the business where you used to work? If you have not already been made redundant, this could form part of your exit negotiations. Have you seen something on holidays – a product, service or business – that you could not find at home? Perhaps you could adapt this idea for Irish customers?

And the most obvious way of copying a good idea is by franchising it. Lots of businesses, especially service businesses, grow by franchising their business idea, the underlying systems and brand to other people.

Creating ideas is where the true entrepreneur comes in – they see opportunities where no one else can. Developing your idea to its fullest potential involves creative thinking. Be careful – it's easy to be creative and to come up with clever ideas for possible businesses. But, once the creative burst is over, look at your ideas again in the cold light of day and see whether they really stack up. That's where your market research comes into its own.

If you can identify a sector that still thrives, even in a downturn, and can find a place for yourself in that sector, then not only will you be creating a business for now but you should be creating one that will flourish when the good times return. Examples of these kinds of business sectors include the green or environmental sector, education and IT.

Start, Buy or Franchise?

In most cases, people considering self-employment think first about starting their own business – but there are alternatives.

Buying an existing business can be a sensible alternative to starting a business from scratch. The main advantage is that the business has existing products, markets, customers, staff and so on. Thus you don't have to build them all up from scratch yourself. The disadvantage is that, usually, a considerable investment is needed to acquire the business, and more money may have to be added to develop it further.

And, just like when buying a second-hand car, it is also important to know why the business is being sold. The key issue is the value of the business – what you will have to pay for it – which is determined by its potential for earning profit in the future. Remember that previous years' profits are a guide to future earnings but cannot always be relied on, especially in a downturn.

Across the world, there are thousands of franchised businesses, covering almost every industry. When you buy a franchise, you buy the right to use a specific trademark or business concept, which has been tested in practice. The chief benefit is that you are able to capitalise on the business format, trade name and support system provided by the franchisor.

In return for an initial upfront fee and ongoing fees for the right to the franchise, the franchisor supplies a detailed operational manual, which sets out exactly how to run the franchise. It is also usual for franchisees to pay into a co-operative national advertising and promotional fund, which benefits all franchises through increased exposure to the common trade name.

The advantages of buying a franchise are:

- A much lower failure rate than other start-up businesses, since most of the problems have been discovered and solved
- A complete package including trademarks, easy access to an established product, a proven marketing method, equipment, stock, financial and accounting systems, on-going training and support, research and development, sales and marketing assistance, and planning and forecasting.

Franchises are not for everyone – but they do offer an alternative entry route to self-employment, with a lower risk threshold. Since the business concept has already been tested by other franchisees, there's less risk of failure. This is particularly important if this is your first venture into business for yourself.

Starting a new business from scratch is the conventional path to self-employment. It means coming up with the idea, planning it, financing it and then executing it. In most cases, you will be forced far beyond your comfort zone into areas that you know nothing about. And, because of that, it's risky – if you don't know what you are doing, the risks of making a mistake, especially a fatal mistake, are greater. International studies repeatedly show that, typically, 50 per cent of start-ups fail within the first few years.

But it's not all doom and gloom either. Thousands of people start new businesses every day – and about half of them survive and succeed. Those who do succeed usually attribute this to planning. So don't dismiss starting from scratch – but don't underestimate the challenges it poses either!

Evaluating Your Idea

The key to achieving sales is the match between your idea and the needs of the marketplace. The key questions here are:

- Will anybody want to buy my product or service?
- Who will buy it?
- Why? (and why from me?)
- When? (and how often?)
- Where?

The first question is the most important – and it is the one that is most often skipped over by would-be entrepreneurs in their rush to get to market. That way lies failure – sometimes fast, sometimes slow, but always certain.

The only way that you can answer the question of whether anybody will want to buy your product or service is by asking people – that is, by doing market research.

You need to be very objective and hard-nosed about your market research. Don't assume – check things out for yourself. Don't accept what people tell you – again, check it out. Don't let your passion for your product or service and your enthusiasm blind you to the reality of the marketplace – that perhaps your product or service is not wanted, or not wanted in that shape or size or format, or at that price, or in that location – whatever. And the only way you will find out is by asking people – your potential customers.

The first step in market research is to put together some statistics on the market that you are aiming for. For example:

- How big is the market?
- Where is it?
- Is it growing or contracting?

The Central Statistics Office produces Small Area Population Statistics, which will give you demographic information right down to the level of townlands. Also check with your local library – or the main library in your nearest town – and with your county or city enterprise board, chamber of commerce or other business-support organisations locally – they may have done some research in the area or be aware of research done locally that may be useful in filling in some of the picture for you.

You should have some intuitive idea of the customers your business is going to target. Use your market research to confirm this.

Can you write a profile of your typical customer? Can you distinguish your customers from those of your competitors? How can you identify your customers from among the many people in the town, city or country in which you are located? This is critical because, unless you can identify your customers, how will you know how to reach them? What are the defining characteristics of your customers:

- Are they old or young?
- Are they rich or poor?
- Do they have children? If so, are they babies or teenagers?
- Where do they live?
- What kinds of cars do they drive?
- Do they take foreign holidays? How often? And where?

- Do they use the Internet?
- Have they credit cards? Which ones? How much do they use them? And for what?
- Do they buy locally or do they buy by post or over the telephone?
- Do they respond to television advertising?

There are hundreds of questions that you can ask about your customers that will help you to define who they are. Without this customer profile firmly in your mind, most of your marketing effort will be no more than random shots into the dark.

Your market research should also help you to identify your competition, which can be local, national or, increasingly, international. It can be direct (someone who provides the same or a very similar product or service) or indirect (someone who provides something completely different, but which takes potential spending power from your customer). Answer these questions to identify and assess your competitors:

- What are the alternatives to your products or services?
- Who makes or sells these alternatives?
- What range of products or services do they have?
- What kinds of choices do they offer customers?
- How broad is their range?
- What are their target groups?
- What are their future prospects?
- What are they good at and what are they not so good at?

The key to winning at competition – especially indirect competition – is to understand your customers and why they buy (or don't buy) from you.

Note that market research should be an ongoing process. It should not stop after the business has started but should become an integral part of your business.

Stages in a Start-Up

If you decide to proceed with your business idea and to start a business, you will need to:

- Open a bank account
- Decide on a legal structure
- Register for tax
- Choose advisers
- Prepare financial projections
- Get the necessary finance
- Write a business plan.

At least one bank account is an essential for any business, however small. Don't be tempted to run your business through your own personal bank account 'until it gets off the ground'. That is a recipe for disaster. Open a separate bank account for your business as soon as (or before) you begin to trade.

You automatically become a sole trader by starting up a business, since this form of legal structure requires almost nothing by way of legal formality. A further advantage of being a sole trader is that apart from normal tax returns, which every business must make, a sole trader is not required to make public any information on their business.

However, the downside – and it is a very significant downside – is that sole traders have unlimited liability. This means that, if the business fails, all your personal assets can be called upon to pay off any money the business owes – ultimately, you could lose your house.

A partnership is an agreement between two or more people to go into business together. Like a sole trader, there's little or no formality involved. However, in a partnership each partner is liable for all the liabilities of the business. If the business fails and your partner(s) abandon(s) you, you could be left to pay for everything out of your own pocket. Before entering a partnership, decide whether you trust your partner(s)-to-be with everything you own – because that's effectively what you will be doing. In addition, write down and have all the partners sign a document setting out how the business is to be financed, how profits and losses are to be shared, and what will happen if one of the partners decides to leave. These are important points. Failure to agree on them at an early stage can lead to difficulty later.

A limited company is a legal entity separate from its shareholders. The shareholders are only liable, in the event of the business becoming unable to pay its debts, for any amount outstanding on their shareholdings. This protects whatever assets you own that you have not committed to the business – for example, your home, savings, car and other possessions – unless you have given a personal guarantee to a bank for the business's borrowings or a court finds you at fault in the collapse of the company.

The cost of forming a limited company depends on whether you do the work yourself or ask an accountant, solicitor, or company formation agent to do it for you. Understandably, using a professional adds to the cost, although you can do it yourself for as little as €60.

If your application to form a company is accepted, the registrar will issue a Certificate of Incorporation. Only after its issue and the first meeting of the board of directors of the company may the company begin to trade. Again, it's important that shareholders sign an agreement similar to the partnership agreement described above.

Note that, if you plan to run your business under a name other than your own (sole trader), the name(s) of the partners (partnership) or the company's name (limited company), then you must register the trading name with the Companies Registration Office.

The Revenue Commissioners now use a single form to register a business for the many taxes to which it is liable. Form TR1 applies to individuals and Form TR2 to companies.

Your business's PAYE/PRSI registration number, its value added tax (VAT) registration number and its corporation tax number should be the same, though it has nothing to do with the company's registered number, which is issued by the Companies Registration Office when the company is formed.

As a first step to understanding your responsibilities under the tax legislation, download Revenue's *Starting in Business* guide (reference IT 48) and *VAT for Small Businesses* (IT 49) from its website (www.revenue.ie).

Employers must register for PAYE when they pay remuneration exceeding a rate of €8 a week (€36 a month) to a full-time employee or €2 a week (€9 a month) to an individual with other employment – in other words, *all* employees, including directors.

You must register your business for VAT as soon as its taxable supplies (that is, your business transactions that are liable to VAT) exceed or become likely to exceed the limits for registration. The current (April 2009) limits are:

- €75,000, where the supplies are of goods
- €37,500, where the supplies are of services.

In certain circumstances you may register for VAT before you begin to trade or while your turnover is below the limits for registration. Doing so allows you to reclaim VAT paid on purchases of goods and may be of advantage to you. However, voluntary registration for VAT should not be done without professional advice. Consult your accountant and/or local tax office for further information.

The Revenue Commissioners require all businesses to keep 'sufficient' records of transactions to allow the correct tax to be calculated. You must keep:

- Details of all receipts and expenses incurred in the course of your business and of what they relate to
- Details of all sales and purchases made in the course of the trade, if you deal in goods
- All other supporting documents.

As you start in business, you will need two key advisers: an accountant and a solicitor. Under pressure in setting up your new business, you may be tempted to avoid finding either of these two. Not doing so saves you time and possibly money, both of which are important in a start-up situation, but it could cost you dearly later on. Their experience and expertise in dealing with other start-ups may save you hours of time and hundreds or even thousands of Euros. If they are the right advisers for you, they will be able to assist your enterprise with timely and constructive advice – take it and use it!

In choosing advisers, look for:

- Membership of the appropriate professional body
- Experience in the type of business or at least in the business area in which you intend to operate
- Adequate resources to meet your needs
- People you can trust and work easily with.

If you do not know a suitable accountant, check the *Golden Pages* or contact one of the following:

- Association of Chartered Certified Accountants (www.accaglobal.com)
- Institute of Certified Public Accountants in Ireland (www.cpaireland.ie)
- Institute of Chartered Accountants in Ireland (www.icai.ie).

Unlike an accountant, a solicitor has no statutory duties in relation to a company. You will, however, need a solicitor for the following:

- To sign a statutory declaration when you are forming your company
- To check out the lease of any premises you decide to buy or rent
- To prepare employment contracts for you and your staff
- To draft or review contracts that you enter into with customers or suppliers.

In addition, from time to time, you may require advice on legal issues.

If you do not know a suitable solicitor, look in the *Golden Pages* or contact the Law Society of Ireland (www. lawsociety.ie).

Loneliness and a sense of isolation are the two most common complaints among entrepreneurs (after the difficulty of getting someone to finance their business!). That's why it is so important to have the support of your family. But sometimes you need more than support – you need someone who has been there, done that; someone who has experienced what you are going through. This is where a mentor can be helpful.

A mentor is an experienced businessperson who makes available their experience and expertise to small businesses, usually for very modest reward. Most mentors are 'putting something back into the system'. There are several mentor schemes available – from Enterprise Ireland and the county and city enterprise boards – or, sometimes, your bank may be able to suggest a suitable mentor.

The business plan is the most misunderstood element of starting a business. Too many people believe that the entrepreneur only needs to prepare a business plan when he or she is looking to raise finance. That's not true. Certainly, it is nearly impossible to raise finance without a business plan, but the real value of the business plan rests in the thinking about the business that is necessary before you can write down what you plan to do.

Once you have done the necessary market research for the project and have decided to go ahead and start your own business, your next step is to write a business plan that summarises the following points about your proposed business:

- Where it has come from
- Where it is now
- Where it is going in the future
- How it intends to get there

- How much money it needs to fulfil its plans
- What makes it likely to succeed?
- What threats or disadvantages must be overcome on the way?

The business plan can range in length from a few typed sheets of paper to several hundred pages. However, since professional readers of business plans – bankers, venture capitalists and county and city enterprise board officers – are offered more business plans than they can intelligently digest, the more concise the business plan, the more likely it is to be read.

You can write a business plan to help you run the business; for a potential business partner; investors; banks; the county and city enterprise boards or other support organisations. Each type of business plan is slightly different – but only in emphasis, not in its core job of explaining the proposed direction of the business.

Typically, the structure of a business plan is as follows:

- Executive summary: this is the first part of a business plan to be read – and, because of its importance, the last to be written. Here, in less than a page, you should summarise the key points of your plan
- Introduction and background: this is the start of the business plan proper. Here, you set out the basic information that a reader will want to know about the business: the purpose of the plan; business name and contact details; whether it is in operation or has yet to start; the business objective; the product or service range
- Project outline: here you go into more detail about the business, giving the reader a sense of what you are setting out to achieve

- Ownership, management and employment: since you are personally one of the critical success factors of the business, readers of the business plan will want to know about you – and your team (if any). This is not a place for boasting – you should simply explain why you believe that you are a good bet to make a success of the business, based on your (relevant) education, work and other experience. Your business partners (if any) should also complete this section. And, since most of the State agencies – Enterprise Ireland and the county and city enterprise boards, for example – are focused on job creation, it makes sense to tell them about the extent to which the business will contribute to job creation
- Markets and marketing strategy: this is a critical section that will be read carefully by any investor, banker or grant-giver. Because readers are unlikely to be familiar with the specific market(s) into which your business proposes to sell, you need to set the scene for them by providing an overview of the market, including (if appropriate) its place in the overall economy or industry sector; key indicators of size, value, customer numbers, growth, etc.; target groups and customers; competitors; the business's key competitive advantage(s); the business's marketing strategy; and the business's distribution strategy and route to market
- Production: again, because readers may have no experience of the business market, you need to explain: the product or service; how it is made and delivered; the experience you have with the process; what equipment the process needs (this should tie in with the financial projections later); how you will assure quality; where you will source supplies. If there is too much detail, don't dwell on it here; put it in an appendix

- Financial: most readers of business plans not only have a financial background, they are preparing to invest in the business. Therefore, they pay special attention to the financial section. Here, you set out a summary of your financial projections – profit and loss account, balance sheet and cash flow (see later for advice on the detailed projections). These numbers should reflect the plan described in earlier sections. Whatever your own background, and whether you have prepared the projections personally (many entrepreneurs rely on their accountant or adviser for this), you need to be sufficiently sure of your financial projections to be able to withstand severe questioning (think of the mauling some participants on *Dragon's Den* receive!). No one will invest in or lend money to your business if you appear to be incapable of controlling it
- Funding proposal: this is the important bit from your point of view. Here you lay out your stall. You have already explained what the business does, the market, the product, the financial projections; now you are saying: 'I need €xxk, made up as follows. I have €xxk of my own. I have tied down €xxk more from these sources. I need €xxk, please.' You must be very sure of your calculations here. If €10k is needed, say so. If it's €12k, say that. The €2k difference will assume a magnitude out of all proportion to reality when the business runs out of money and investors or lenders will not support it further because they no longer trust you
- Detailed financial projections: almost an appendix, this is where the real number-crunching is put – out of the way at the back. The critical part here is your assumptions, which should be explicitly stated. You can expect to be quizzed on these when you make a

presentation of your business plan to a county or city enterprise board or a bank.

FURTHER READING AND INFORMATION

More information on all of the stages of starting a business:

Immink, R. and O'Kane, B. (2001), *Starting Your Own Business: A Workbook*, Dublin: Oak Tree Press (by and published by Oak Tree Press: www.oaktreepress.com).

Start Your Own Business courses offered by the county and city enterprise boards (www.enterpriseboards.ie).

The website www.startingabusinessinireland.com

In addition, key sources of assistance for start-ups in Ireland include:

AIB Bank: www.aib.ie

Bank of Ireland: www.bankofireland.ie

Bord Bia: www.bordbia.ie

Business incubation centres

Central Statistics Office: www.cso.ie

Companies Registration Office: www.cro.ie

County and city enterprise boards: www.enterpriseboards.ie

Crafts Council of Ireland: www.ccoi.ie

Enterprise Ireland: www.enterprise-ireland.com

Fáilte Ireland: www.failteireland.ie

FÁS: www.fas.ie

First Step: www.first-step.ie

Health and Safety Authority: www.hsa.ie

Irish Franchise Association:
www.irishfranchiseassociation.com

LEADER+ companies: www.irishleadernetwork.org

National Standards Authority of Ireland: www.nsai.ie

Patents Office: www.patentsoffice.ie

Revenue Commissioners: www.revenue.ie

Shannon Development: www.shannondev.ie

SmallBusinessCan: www.smallbusinesscan.com

Údarás na Gaeltachta: www.udaras.ie

Ulster Bank: www.ulsterbank.ie

7

Educational Opportunities

Patrick McGuinness

Exploring the Options Open to You

It is well known that one of the best ways to improve your individual wealth, even in these difficult times, is through continuous learning. The formula is simple – up your skills and you open up opportunities.

In its report looking at our economy over the next decade, the Government Expert Group on Future Skills Needs states: 'Employees in all jobs will be increasingly required to acquire a range of generic and transferable skills including people-related and conceptual/thinking skills. Work will be less routine, with a requirement for flexibility, continuous learning, and individual initiative and judgement.'

Being made redundant can give you a chance to think about whether you would like to change career, develop new skills, recharge the batteries and move on to pastures new. You might feel you need to return to education. This does not have to be full time so you can continue to seek employment. There are now many opportunities for adults to undertake courses and training programmes – from acquiring basic skills (literacy and numeracy skills, for example) to degree or even postgraduate courses. These are accessible to all. The Internet provides great access to what is available and the choices are enormous.

The following are just a few examples:

- Acquiring some computer skills
- Increasing your understanding of IT
- Developing supervisory skills
- Learning basic foreign language skills
- Developing your ability to communicate.

These and more courses are available from the vocational education committees (VECs), FÁS and the institutes of technology. There are also courses that relate to specific industries, for example, a course on good manufacturing practice for the pharmaceutical industry.

You may have been an experienced manager in a functional area such as production or finance and you may want to develop a broader business perspective. There are advanced courses to degree and master's degree levels available from the institutes of technology and universities, collectively known as higher education institutes (HEIs). One of the main problems faced by potential participants is which course to choose!

Many people can be intimidated by the prospect of returning to education, particularly if they have been away from formal education for a long time. Hours of boredom in school, stuck in classrooms studying subjects that they had no interest in leaves its mark. It can be hard to appreciate that learning in a classroom can actually be a fun and rewarding experience.

Educational Opportunities

Adult learners enjoy advantages over young people. You will likely be studying something you are interested in and perhaps you already have experience related to the area and know how the learning can be applied in real life. This provides motivation, which is very important to those undertaking any course or indeed any challenge.

It might be worth considering taking on a short course first to give you a taste of what it is like to resume education. These courses, such as those that can be found on the nightcourse website (www.nightcourses.com) are designed in such a manner as to take full account of peoples' fears. The tutors also understand the different needs of adults and are trained to support participants, especially in the early stages. They appreciate that people may lack confidence and need time to adjust.

The environment allows individuals to progress at their own rate. There will also be support from other participants who are in a similar position.

Apart from the educational benefits, courses also provide a great opportunity to socialise and interact with other people who have similar concerns and worries. Lasting friendships are often formed.

Studying at a Higher Education Institute

Why Consider Third-Level Education as a Mature Student?

A mature student is any candidate who is 23 years of age on 1 January of the year of entry (or re-entry) to an approved course in a recognised higher education institute. Mature students enter third-level education for a variety of reasons:

- To complete their education and get a degree
- To further develop an interest that they have always had in a given subject
- To improve their job prospects
- To retrain for another career
- To develop their social and personal skills.

Returning to education after a break or entering it for the first time as a mature student is becoming increasingly popular and indeed desirable. The mature student brings life experience allied with determination and focus, all of which are conducive to successful learning. The 'mature student' very often becomes the 'ideal student'.

What Sorts of Courses are there?

Those candidates entering third level for the first time will enter at undergraduate level to do a certificate, diploma or degree course. A certificate generally involves one to two years of study. If you desire and if your results allow it, you can progress to diploma level after which a degree is possible. The degree usually entails three to five years of study (depending on what route you take). Postgraduate opportunities are open to candidates who already hold an initial degree, although applications are sometimes considered from those with substantial relevant experience in their chosen area of study.

How Can I Find Out What's on Offer?

Full course details are available from each individual HEI. These details are updated annually, and are available in their prospectuses and online as well.

Educational Opportunities

How Do I Apply?

Most HEIs require you to apply via the Central Applications Office (CAO) (www.cao.ie) though some colleges require you to apply directly, and still others require you to do both. Many institutions also require you to attend an interview. Each institution has an admissions office, and staff are always happy to answer queries from prospective students. Though the common deadline for mature applicants applying through the CAO is 1 February in the year of entry, it is important to note that deadlines can vary too. Please check with your chosen college for their entry requirements.

Can I Apply for any Course I Want?

Some restrictions may apply in the case of applications from mature applicants or in relation to certain courses. Again, the admissions office in the HEI you are interested in can confirm the specific requirements.

How Can I Find out if Third-Level Education Is Right for Me?

If this is your first time to enter third-level study, you might want to consider some sort of foundation or access course. Many HEIs run their own such courses and local VECs also run courses for mature applicants.

What Help Is Available to Mature Students at Third Level?

Most HEIs have a dedicated mature student officer who will be able to tell you what services and supports are available to mature students. These can include academic supports, counselling, careers advice, health services, accommodation, crèche facilities, disability services and chaplaincy.

Many HEIs also run dedicated orientation or induction programmes for mature students, which take place before you begin your chosen course and are designed to help in the transition to third-level study.

Support is also provided for people with physical or learning disabilities, and will typically include learning support, access to specialised software and specific individual student support where necessary.

What Is Available Outside of Higher Education Institutes?

AONTAS is the Irish National Association of Adult Education. It has about five hundred statutory and voluntary members, all of which provide education opportunities. Community education has developed strongly in recent years and it is estimated that there are over one thousand groups providing learning and development opportunities to a diverse range of people. AONTAS believes that people learn continuously throughout their lives in formal or informal settings: at home, in the workplace, in the community or in learning centres and institutions. No matter when or at what level you finished your initial formal education, you have been learning new things since.

According to AONTAS, an adult learner is someone who:

- Decides to do a part-time course in a local community centre or group
- Left school at an early age but has returned to learning to gain a formal qualification
- Is improving his or her reading and writing skills through one-to-one classes
- Undertakes a course to learn how to use a computer

- Learns on the job in a training course
- Never has the chance to go to college after school so has enrolled as a mature student
- Has updated his or her skills to improve career or employment prospects
- Learns a new language or undertakes a hobby course
- Participates in social or leisure courses
- Participates in active retirement activities.

Have you done any of the above? If so, you are an adult learner. And you're in the company of thousands of adults throughout Ireland. AONTAS also has a very good website (www.aontas.com) where it has a number of case studies of real people who made the leap into further education. These are worthwhile reading.

FÁS, the Training and Employment Authority, provides some 400 courses annually throughout the country and has a range of online courses also. Checking out what FÁS has to offer is a good starting point. This can be done at any of their 60 offices around the country. See also www.fas.ie.

As mentioned earlier, VECs, which are responsible for vocational and community schools, are very big providers of education. They offer a wide range of full-time and part-time courses through their Vocational Training Opportunities Schemes (VTOS).

These programmes are excellent for adults who need to return to full-time education without losing their social welfare benefits, provided they pass a means test. As already covered in Chapter 3, you may also be able to avail of travel and meal allowances, free books and exemption from fees. Certain conditions apply to these schemes and your local social welfare office will furnish you with details of eligibility.

The types of courses available include a two-year Leaving Certificate course, a fast-track course on new technology such as computer-aided design, computer literacy, heritage research, accounts for small business, adventure tourism management and many more (see QualifaX, the National Learners Database: www.qualifax.ie).

VTOS participants may also enrol in Post-Leaving Certificate Courses (PLCs) or Further Education (FE) courses, subject to completing the Leaving Certificate or acquiring suitable work experience. These courses may be used as a ladder to progress into relevant courses at third level, particularly in the institutes of technology. Information on all these courses is available from your local VEC.

Generally, mature applicants are assessed on grounds other than the Leaving Certificate results. Universities usually look for some evidence of ability to follow and benefit from the proposed study programme. The larger VECs also provide a guidance service to adults wishing to undertake courses and it is wise to avail of this service where possible.

Getting Qualifications

Today, certificates of qualification as evidence of your skills are sought by most employers. Therefore, it is useful to understand what sort of award or qualification you will receive on completion of the course you are considering undertaking.

For instance, the Further Education and Training Awards Council provides a qualification commonly known as FETAC. Most VEC and most courses provided by Bord Iascaigh Mhara

(BIM), CERT, FÁS and Teagasc meet FETAC's requirements. There are several private providers also.

Universities and institutes of technology are gearing up to provide more courses for adults and operate under the Higher Education and Training Awards Council (HETAC), which awards qualifications at all levels of higher education and training up to Ph.D. level. Many of these courses are in modular form, which means you can graduate to certificate and then to diploma level, before moving on, if you wish, to degree level. This allows you to progress at your own pace. Each of the colleges provides information about what is covered in each course and where job opportunities exist when you are qualified. There are also private colleges, such as All Hallows College and Dorset College in Dublin, Galway Business School, Mary Immaculate College in Limerick and many others, offering a whole range of courses. These tend to be more expensive but should not be ruled out as many specialise in courses not generally available elsewhere.

Unemployed adults may be entitled to retain their social welfare benefits while attending a full-time course in a HEI or doing a course through the VTOS.

Distance Learning

There are a growing number of online distance learning courses that allow you to study from home. Some people may find this difficult depending on their circumstances. For others, it is the ideal solution. Providers of such courses include:

- Quinn Business School (www.ucd.ie/quinnschool) – offers business-related distance learning courses

- Kilroy's College (www.kilroyscollege.ie) – a private college that provides many courses in home study
- Daycourses.com (www.daycourses.com) – contains a complete guide to full-time and part-time third-level education courses in Ireland
- Oscail (www.oscail.ie), the National Distance Education Centre of Ireland – offers the opportunity to receive an Irish university qualification through distance learning
- FÁS Net College (www.ecollege.ie) – provides a range of elearning courses aimed at employers, employees and unemployed people
- The National Extension College (www.nec.ac.uk) – an educational charity dedicated to providing learning opportunities for all. It offers a wide range of distance learning courses for adults, including GCSEs, A-Levels, basic skills courses, child-care courses and much more
- The National College of Ireland (NCI) (www.ncirl.ie/default.asp) – offers a range of online courses
- Nightcourses.com (www.nightcourses.com) – contains a searchable database of national evening courses, facilitating distance education and lifelong learning
- CollegesWeb.com (www.webcolleges.com) – the aim of this website is to provide individuals who wish to further their education with options that are available in Ireland
- The Open University (www.open.ac.uk) – offers over 360 undergraduate and postgraduate courses and is one of the biggest providers of distance education courses. There is generally back-up, with collective tutorials locally in designated centres, and you can send in queries about any aspect of the course.

Funding

For adult learners attending courses that are approved by the Department of Education and Science for the Higher Education Grants Scheme there are two principal forms of assistance:

- Back to Education Allowance
- Higher Education Grant.

Back to Education Allowance is an educational opportunities scheme for unemployed people, lone parents and people with disabilities who are getting certain payments from the Department of Social and Family Affairs. The Higher Education Grant is for mature students who are at least 23 years of age on 1 January of the year of entry or re-entry to an approved third-level course in an approved institution and is subject to a means test. Details of the Back to Education Allowance Scheme are available from the local office of the Department of Social and Family Affairs (www.welfare.ie). Details of the Higher Education Grants are available from the Department of Education and Science (www.education.ie).

A *Guide for Mature Students on Entry into Full-Time Third Level Courses,* published by the Department of Education and Science, is available free to any interested parties.

Further education is a rewarding experience and will lead to opportunities and new possibilities in the future. Even in these difficult times, education is now seen as a right for all and not just for the few. Availing of the opportunities out there is an investment in you – and there can be no better investment.

8

Seeking Job Opportunities Abroad

Dermot Killen and Patrick McGuinness

Like so many others during the era of the Celtic Tiger, you may never have given a moment's thought to being unemployed. While you may understandably prefer to continue to live and work in Ireland, suitable job opportunities may not be available when you need them. Furthermore, employment prospects in the medium term may not be too promising either.

Faced with this reality, you may wish to consider employment opportunities abroad in order to use your talents and realise your professional and life ambitions. As we all know, going overseas to work is nothing new and can be considered a viable option at any time. In addition, the fact that you used your initiative and went abroad, together with the nature of the work itself, may well serve to enhance your CV in the eyes of some prospective employers in the future. A recent study by HSBC of people living overseas identified that:

- Singapore, the United Arab Emirates (UAE) and the United States are the three best expatriate locations
- The United Kingdom and France are amongst the lowest rated destinations, scoring poorly on their levels of luxury and accommodation.

Europe is a popular destination overall in terms of the length of time expatriates stay there. Over three quarters (82 per cent) of expatriates living in the Netherlands have been there for three or more years, followed by Germany (77 per cent) and Spain (76 per cent).

Interestingly, Ireland and New Zealand have the greatest percentage of global travellers, with over three quarters (80 per cent) of respondents originally from both countries stating that they had been living away from home for longer than three years.

Preparing to Move

Opportunities to work abroad generally fall into two categories. The first of these is the category of a project-based or short-term assignment, lasting for a period of eighteen months or less. It could, for example, include being seconded for a particular project or working for charities such as Concern, Trócaire and Goal.

During this time, you would relocate on a temporary basis with the option, perhaps, of extended weekend trips back to Ireland at regular intervals to keep in touch with family and friends, and to continue your search for suitable employment when your assignment or project comes to an end.

The second category – emigrating to a country of your choice – requires you to make a more fundamental commitment in that, from the outset, your intention is one of 'setting down roots' and building a new life.

Indeed, it is conceivable that a project or short-term assignment – even in a country from which extended weekend trips home may simply not be a practical option – could provide you with the opportunity to 'try it out', while keeping your options open in terms of returning to Ireland, staying on or even moving elsewhere.

If you are thinking of emigrating, the more preparation you do, the better. Do you have to emigrate alone? Is it possible that there are other people interested in doing so as well? Check around with your friends and acquaintances. It may easier to do so in a small group who can look out for one another, share accommodation expenses and so on.

Let us now turn to some of the issues you would need to address if planning to work abroad.

Location

What's your preferred location? Where might you like to be? Where are you likely to find the opportunity to realise your dreams with your new life abroad? This sort of reflection can guide you in your location research and ensure that, wherever in the world you choose, the opportunities, facilities and services to which you aspire will be available. You may have been on holiday abroad and found somewhere that appears ideal. Be careful. Being on holidays in a particular location is one thing; working there may be something else altogether.

If you are a native English speaker, for example, you might initially consider those countries where you will immediately understand the spoken language and feel reasonably comfortable with its culture, for instance, the United

Kingdom, New Zealand, Australia, Canada and the United States.

Are you fluent in another language or, if not currently fluent (orally and in the written word), are there steps you can take to quickly remedy this? For example, you might concentrate initially on common conversational phrases, such as greetings, asking directions and making simple purchases, that will assist with essential needs when you arrive. In such circumstances, on arrival in the country, intensive language training for you (and your family, where appropriate) would be essential.

In some cases, your (future) employer may cover, in whole or in part, the cost of further language training for you and your family, although this is rare. Take advantage of this benefit if it is available. In any event, even if you yourself are obliged to cover this expense following your arrival in the country, it will be a worthwhile investment, helping you (and your family) to become assimilated more quickly.

In terms of increasing your options further, is there a language you have always wanted to learn, but never seemed to have the time? If there is – and a really good knowledge of it could help provide a key to your future – are you prepared to apply yourself right away and start learning as an essential part of your pre-departure preparation?

Jobs Abroad

Having narrowed your choice of potential destinations, a critical task is to establish the nature and extent of employment opportunities available for an individual with your qualifications, experience and skill set. Are your qualifications recognised in the prospective country or will you have to undertake a conversion course in order for them to be accepted? This can be expensive in some cases and may, at best, delay you getting employment. If your qualifications are acceptable, are they in demand?

Do bear in mind that, if you intend to travel with a spouse or partner, his or her qualifications and skill set may prove very advantageous in terms of obtaining a working visa. Above all, make sure that you are allowed to work in the country that you wish to move to and that any working restrictions currently in place are not insurmountable.

Even if there is a demand for people with your background, how realistic is it that you will secure employment and how long might the job search take once you arrive in the country? Might it be possible to begin the job search immediately, using the Internet to identify potential employers, recruitment agencies or executive search firms, and government-linked agencies?

Another important consideration is accessibility to the country. Do low-cost airlines fly to the country? It may be possible to commute, at least initially, on a weekly basis.

The more you know, the better able you will be to choose the right option for you.

Potential Income and Tax Matters

Once you are satisfied that your destination of choice has suitable opportunities, you will need to consider your potential earning power, at least in the short to medium term. What are you likely to earn on a weekly, monthly or annual basis?

As each country has its own taxation system, you will need to establish how that will affect your net or after-tax income. You will also need to establish the extent of local taxes and charges, which would further reduce your disposable income.

The major accountancy practices have international links and one of these or, alternatively, one of the specialist human resource or compensation and benefits' consultancies may be worth a visit, albeit at a fee, to provide you with the relevant information. The advice should provide some indication of the standard of living (relative to your current circumstances) your net income will yield, taking into account the cost of accommodation, food, education expenses for children, health cover and so on.

If you wish to continue being treated as an Irish 'resident' for a period of time following your departure, you will need a good understanding of the tax system at home and how it may apply. Also, it is worthwhile establishing the nature of the tax agreements between the countries so as to ensure you are not taxed on the double.

In such circumstances, to ensure that you minimise your tax liabilities while remaining tax compliant, specialist advice may not only prove very helpful, it may end up saving you a considerable sum of money.

Visas and Permissions

You need to know whether you will require a visa to move to your chosen country before you arrive or whether you can arrange employment and residency visas once you get there.

You should be aware of your legal obligations in terms of getting permission to enter and reside in a given country before you even set out. Bear in mind that if you fall foul of the national laws of your host country, you may be fined, imprisoned and/or deported, depending on the severity of the relevant legislation.

Seeking Job Opportunities Abroad

Initial Visit

You may wish to consider making a 'preliminary' visit to your preferred destination before finally making the decision to move there. With careful planning, you might consider going alone initially to allow you to focus on the job search, possibly attend pre-arranged interviews, identify potential accommodation and schools, experience the cost of living and so on.

Your family might then join you for a 'working holiday' over a two- or three-week period to give them an opportunity to make their own assessment of living there.

By way of preparation, become familiar with the general geographic and economic factors that have shaped your host country and its people. Learn something about its basic history. Become familiar with recent events which are important to its people. Take an interest in subjects that will make the host country and its people seem three dimensional so you can more easily establish relationships with host nationals.

Key areas of attention include learning how to make introductions and greetings properly, understanding food habits, mores about drinking and smoking, conversation topics, relations between the sexes and the culture of gift-giving. The more you know, the more prepared you will be.

Before you leave for your visit, talk to business colleagues, family and friends to try and establish whether they have any contacts in your chosen destination who may be of potential help to you. Do not be afraid to ask to be put in touch with them. Once you have arrived in the country, make sure you contact them – many, if not all of them, will be only too willing to share their knowledge and experience with you and your family and pave the way to further useful contacts.

Make sure that you retain a list of contacts. This will provide the basis for your 'network' in the event that your visit is deemed a success and a more permanent move is the likely outcome.

Both you and your family will return from that visit with greater knowledge and awareness, and better positioned to make an informed decision on whether to remain in Ireland or to continue with your preparations.

Retaining Your Home in Ireland

Now that the decision to depart has been made, if you own or have a stake in a property in Ireland, consider your plans for this holding. Will you consider renting it out or possibly even selling it? Any decision will be influenced by your personal finances, the likely demand for and selling price of your property, and whether your move abroad will be temporary or permanent.

It is worth bearing in mind that property is (potentially) a valuable asset and consideration of any taxation implications – for example, Capital Gains Tax liabilities – may well have an influence on your approach.

Financial Planning

Before you move out, make sure you have sufficient money in the bank at home to tide you over once you arrive. This will make sure you have a financial lifeline while you are settling in, looking for a job or finalising your employment arrangements.

Financial planning can be technical and tedious but is critical when you move abroad. Making solid financial preparations will minimise your worries while making the transition a much easier proposition. In addition, do not forget to establish whether the PRSI contributions you have already made in Ireland are transferable to your new country through international agreements Ireland may have with other nations.

If at all possible, try to ensure that your total weekly or monthly expenditure does not exceed your net income for the same period. While this might well prove to be a real challenge, it will protect any capital sum which either accompanied you on your journey or is secured in an Irish bank. This sum can then be used to purchase your new home.

Finding a Home

Rather than commit yourself to the purchase of property upon your arrival or shortly thereafter, you might prefer to rent accommodation as an initial step. If home ownership (as opposed to renting) is the norm in your new country, renting will provide you (and your family) with breathing space in which to assess how you are settling in and, in addition, some time to look around to allow you to more fully assess the housing market.

If you did not make an initial visit before leaving Ireland, finding short-term rentals online before you go is relatively easy and this base will be very convenient as you begin a proper hunt for your long-term accommodation and home.

Health

Health-care treatment abroad is often a fraught business. Standards can vary, with some countries having a poorly funded health-care system; in other countries a relevant insurance policy is obligatory. In the event that you are unable to obtain any credit in your new host country for your contribution to Ireland's insurance and welfare systems, it is wise to purchase a good international health insurance policy to cover you for a specific period (perhaps a year) for all conceivable circumstances. Continue the policy until your entitlements arising from your new employment begin to provide you and your family with some cover and then reassess your need for additional private cover.

Embassies and Consulates

Ireland may well have an embassy or at least a consular office in the country you're moving to. Ensure you know where these official representatives are located and notify them of your long-term presence in the country. They will be able to render assistance in the event of you finding yourself in a difficult situation or your safety and that of your family is put at risk because of events in the country itself.

Most countries and indeed locations within larger countries will have Irish expatriate organisations that are potentially powerful networks. Look these up before you leave.

Residency and Entry Requirements

Every country has its own requirements. Freedom of movement is guaranteed within the EU and therefore visa requirements are not necessary. Work and residency permits are common for countries outside the EU.

We will examine three countries – Australia (in some depth, because of its long-standing popularity among Irish emigrants), the UAE and Canada – that provide good examples of what is typically involved in moving abroad to work and also illustrate some of the requirements that generally apply. However, it must be emphasised that every country has its own rules and you have to research each country's particular requirements.

Residency and Entry Requirements for Australia

Australia is a very popular destination for Irish people seeking new opportunities abroad. Australia's economy is exceptional in that it is relatively buoyant in the world recession. Australia is also a nation that has substantial Irish roots.

Irish passport holders are required to have a visa to enter Australia. Information on the requirements for entry to Australia is located on the Australian Department of Immigration and Citizenship website (www.immi.gov.au). This website has further details on how to obtain a Working Holiday Visa as well as any additional visa categories that may be applicable to Irish citizens. If you wish to travel to Australia for a period of less than three months, an application can be made online to the Electronic Travel Authority (www.eta.immi.gov.au).

Housing in Australia

Australia has a high standard of living with a whole variety of accommodation options to consider. A wide range of housing is available in larger cities. Architecture has been based largely on European and American styles, but modern housing is distinctly Australian. There are terrace houses and 'Queenslanders', with housing design and style based on the weather and lifestyle of the particular region. Australian houses are famous for having large gardens and many even have swimming pools. A proliferation of local parks and shopping centres help give an excellent quality of life. Towns and regional cities in the country are usually smaller and more separated out. The pace of life in a country town is generally more relaxed and it is less expensive to live there than in a city. There is usually housing available to people who choose to work and live in towns away from popular capital cities.

People living in Australia usually rent before they choose to buy a home or decide where to live. Together with the type of housing, the cost of accommodation varies between the states and the cities of Australia. Many people live in the suburbs of the state capital cities and like to live close to where they work and where they can access community facilities such as schools and leisure areas. You may have to put down a substantial deposit (several months) on any place you rent – so include this in your budget.

Employment in Australia

Depending on your qualifications and area of expertise, employment in Australia is available to a range of skilled and professional people. Nonetheless, it must be borne in mind that no employer will recruit an individual who does not have a valid visa and permission to work in Australia.

The most popular recruitment organisations in Australia include Davidson Recruitment, IPA Personnel and Dekro Recruitment. Australia offers permanent residence visas under four main headings: 1) Skills, 2) Family, 3) Business or Work and 4) Humanitarian. You can also apply for a Temporary Residence Visa pending approval for an application for higher residency rights.

As an Irish citizen is unlikely to seek entry to Australia on humanitarian grounds, let us now consider the other three headings in some detail.

Skills Visas

The skilled stream has several categories, including the Skilled Independent Visa class and similar categories such as the Skilled Sponsored Visa class. The Skilled Independent Visa class is most popular.

To qualify for immigration to Australia under this class, you or your partner must be:

1. Under the age limit of 45 years
2. Possess, as a minimum, competent English
3. Pick an occupation on the Skilled Occupation List (SOL)
4. Possess a minimum of twelve months' work experience in a skilled occupation.

Provided you meet the above criteria, you will be required to undergo a test, the objective of which is to secure sufficient points to reach or exceed the automatic pass mark. The pass mark currently set is available on www.migrationexpert.com/Australia.

The following will be taken into consideration:

• Qualifications
• Work experience
• Occupation
• Age
• English language ability
• Occupation targeting
• Spouse's skills (qualifications, age, work, English language).

Your own profession or that of your spouse will often be the factor determining whether your application fails or succeeds. Having recent work experience in employment on the SOL would be vital and additional points can be accumulated if you have a record of relevant study and languages.

Additional points can also be accumulated if your profession is mentioned on the periodically amended Migration Occupations in Demand List (MODL). Once again, experience is paramount. MODL mentions professions that are understood by the Department of Employment and Workplace Relations as being in demand over the long term. Qualifications must bear relation to your professional occupation as well as being universally recognised degrees. The information on your college's website or the details on your qualification itself should tell you whether it is recognised internationally.

Exceptions can be made for those with a trade or senior executives with a verifiable track record who may not possess formal qualifications. These kinds of applicants can qualify through presenting their relevant work experience in order to secure industry certification, therefore achieving the qualification requirement.

Claimants in professions requiring professional registration, such as dentists or therapists, may need to apply for registration or meet specific requirements prior to submitting a residency application.

Applicants who don't achieve the pass mark for the Skilled Independent Visa class have the option of presenting a sponsored application, either via a member of their family or through a state in which they intend to settle. If there is a qualified family sponsor in Australia, it may be possible to apply under the Skilled Sponsored subclass or the Skilled Regional Sponsored Visa class. This will depend on the address of residence of the intended sponsor.

First cousins and grandparents can also provide sponsorship under the Skilled Regional Sponsored Visa class.

The pass mark in this category is set at a lower level. The Skilled Sponsored Visa class also provides options for those applicants who have an occupation listed as being in demand in a state or territory of Australia. Additional points are available for those applicants nominated by a state or territory.

If your qualifications or experience are such that you do not achieve the minimum pass mark under the Skilled Independent Visa class, but you can meet the minimum requirements and also have a family sponsor living in a designated area such as Sydney, Brisbane, Perth and other specific cities, you may satisfy a sufficient number of the criteria to qualify under the Skilled Regional Sponsored Visa class.

This is a two-step procedure, with a provisional visa issued initially and permanent residence then available when the applicant and his or her family have settled in a designated area in Australia. The applicant must have lived in a designated area for two years and have worked there for a year before being able to apply for the permanent visa.

If your intention is to settle outside the State capitals (except Adelaide), opportunities for regional migration are available under the Skilled Regional Sponsored Visa class. This option involves a two-step procedure through which successful applicants are conferred with a temporary visa that is valid for three years. Recommendation from a state or territory government is essential in order to obtain the first visa. Skilled Regional Sponsored Visa class holders can submit an application for permanent residence after two years' residence in an Australian region, provided that they have worked for at least a year.

The Skill Matching Scheme allows applicants to present their details to the skill-matching database for years, during which time they may receive a nomination to reside in a certain region of Australia. Many of the successful applicants in these particular categories will qualify for residence without the need for a pre-arranged job offer at the time of applying.

The Employer Nomination and the Regional Sponsored Migration schemes can be considered by applicants who have been presented with the opportunity of a highly skilled job that cannot be filled by an Australian citizen or an already permanent resident.

The newly introduced Temporary Recognised Graduate Visa class offers another route for applicants who have graduated from an overseas university or a similar institution and would like to spend a period of time in Australia before finally applying for permanent residence. Applicants in this category must be 30 years of age or under at the time of application, have completed their postgraduate diploma or degree within the last two years from a certified educational facility and have good English. Visa holders will be able to work or study freely within Australia and can apply for a permanent or provisional General Skilled Migration Visa at any time during the validity of their visa.

Family Visas

This category is for those persons who are in a position to be sponsored by a relative or interdependent partner who is either an Australian citizen, a holder of a permanent residence visa or an eligible New Zealand citizen aged over 18 years of age. You can be sponsored if you are a spouse, fiancé(e), child or adopted child, parent, orphan relative, special needs relative, elderly dependent relative or last remaining relative of a qualifying sponsor who is resident in Australia.

Contributory Parent Visas are available for those parents with sufficient capital to contribute to their future health costs in Australia. These visa classes are designed to overcome the otherwise lengthy waiting period currently facing parents wishing to migrate to Australia and are subject to places being available.

Work (Business) Visas

Work Visa or Business (Long Stay) Visa

If you are offered a job in a category where no Australian is available to work and the Australian employer is willing to provide sponsorship, you may be able to apply for a Work Visa. This visa is issued for the duration of the employment contract or four years, whichever is the shorter.

Student Visa

If you are enrolled in a qualifying course at an Australian tertiary institution, you can apply for a Student Visa. This visa allows you to study and to work 20 hours per week. You can only be granted permission to work once you are in Australia and have commenced your course of study. Students who graduate with an Australian degree may be able to apply for permanent 'on-shore' residence visas.

Working Holiday Visa

Citizens of certain countries who are under the age of 30 years may consider obtaining a Young Person's Working Holiday Visa. This visa enables you to work and travel for one year, and allows the holder to work for six months with each employer or undertake a course of study of no more than four months' duration (seventeen weeks of actual study). A second Working Holiday Visa will be available to those who undertake three months of seasonal farm or harvesting work during their first working holiday.

Australian working conditions are controlled by legislation and this has worked well over the years. The average Australian working week is 37 hours. However, this can vary according to employer, the level at which you are employed and the sector of industry in question.

General Residency and Entry Requirements for the United Arab Emirates

Another popular destination that we'll have a brief look at is the United Arab Emirates (UAE). The construction sector in the UAE has made this locale an attractive destination for potential expatriates.

Getting a visa to enter the UAE is usually straightforward, with the authorities issuing the visa within three days. To acquire a visa in the UAE and its seven emirates, you need to have held a passport for a minimum of between two and six months.

Visit Visas

If you simply wish to visit to make arrangements or to come as a tourist, a 'visit visa' is required for you to spend more than a fortnight in the UAE. The Dubai Naturalisation and Residency Department issues visas to foreigners visiting the country. The majority of Visitor Visas are issued through Dubai International Airport and are sometimes referred to as the 'Dubai Visa'. A high proportion of Visitor Visas are conferred during the various events sponsored by the

Dubai Government, including the Dubai Shopping Festival and Dubai Summer Surprises, as the visa requirements are minimised and obtaining a visa is a lot easier.

I recommend that you contact the nearest UAE Embassy or Consulate for the latest information concerning Visit Visas. For other visas contact the Dubai Naturalisation and Residency Administration Department.

Privileged Countries

If you hold British citizenship you are entitled to a free 60-day visa on arrival, with the option to renew it for 30 additional days at a cost of €104 (550 AED).

The UAE gives 33 nations, including Ireland, privileged status on similar terms to British visa applications. These countries include much of Europe, the United States, Canada, Australia and New Zealand.

Residence Visas

Planning for a long-term stay in the United Arab Emirates requires a Residence Visa. The immigration department in the emirate in which you have chosen to stay will be responsible for issuing your resident permit through the sponsor who will be required to endorse your application.

Residence Visas are issued for roughly three years and you will need to take a medical test and acquire a health card. A health card costs around €60 (300 AED) and is renewable annually. This card is issued at the Ministry of Health or else at a private hospital.

A Family Visa is required for families to gain residency. This visa will allow you (assuming you already hold a visa to stay in the country) to sponsor your spouse, children under eighteen and parents. Family visas are made available to those sponsors earning more than €758 (4,000 AED) per month.

Parents are sponsored on a visa provided that the sponsor pays a deposit for each parent and takes out a health insurance policy. This deposit is paid once and will be returned upon the death or departure of the parent.

In the event of overstay, the UAE imposes a levy of €4.75 (25 AED) to €19 (100 AED) per person per day, with further penalties imposed by a judge if the overstay period becomes excessive.

A Summary of Residency and Entry Requirements for Canada

Canada is another frequently discussed destination for Irish people looking for work. To gain long-term residence and to work in Canada, you must be healthy and in possession of a valid passport so that immigration officials can be fully aware of your history at home. If you are in Canada for a short preliminary stay, the immigration department must be satisfied that you will depart Canada at the end of your visit. You must also be sufficiently solvent to finance your stay on these terms. A charge is levied for assessing your application which cannot be refunded, so make sure your eligibility is correct before you apply.

You must have a valid passport for each family member when you make your application and an additional two passport photos for every member of your family. You must provide proof that you have enough money for your visit to Canada. The amount of money varies, dependent on the circumstances of your visit, how long you intend to stay and whether your stay will be in a hotel or with friends or relatives.

The fee per person is levied at €48 ($75 CDN) for a single-entry visa, €96 ($150 CDN) for a multiple-entry visa or €257 ($400) for a family. This is subject to change.

Skilled Workers and Professionals

Immigrants into Canada are favoured by the authorities as permanent residents through criteria such as their education, work experience and how articulate they are in English. This is to ensure that immigrants best suited to making a sustainable livelihood in Canada are given preference.

The Canadian visa authorities look favourably on an immigrant ready with a job offer. If, with the status of a foreign worker, you are resident for one year, the Canadians will likely assess your request. The Canadian authorities change their requirements from time to time so consulting their website (www.cic.gc.ca) is essential. What you will also find on the website is information on the trade and professional categories that are deemed eligible.

Once your application is considered eligible for processing, further criteria are assessed if your application is to be granted. You are obliged to have worked for at minimum one year in ongoing full-time paid employment or the equivalent in part-time continuous employment within the space of the last ten years.

This occupation must be Skill Type 0 under the managerial occupations category or Skill Level A, which is the professional occupations category. Also acceptable is the same work experience in Skill Level B, which deals with technical occupations and skilled trades on the Canadian National Occupational Classification list featured on the Citizenship and Immigration Canada website (www.cic.gc.ca/english/visit/apply-how.asp).

The final stage has more general selection factors that will influence the final decision, such as your age, education, ability to communicate in English (or French), your professional experience, any pre-existing working arrangements and your potential to be financially sustainable in Canada.

There is an eligibility feature and a self-assessment test available on the Citizenship and Immigration website so you can get an idea as to your eligibility.

Temporary Residency

Ireland is among the privileged nations that are eligible under this category. A criminal record is usually grounds enough for an application to be refused. The Citizenship and Immigration website also includes the application guide, information and all the forms you need to fill out.

A medical examination may also be required to enter Canada for temporary and permanent residency. The Canadian Department of Citizenship and Immigration will tell you the exact requirements and will send you instructions. If a medical examination is required, it can cause a delay to your application of almost three months.

Conclusion

The information supplied here about these three popular destinations gives you an indication of the amount of bureaucracy that can arise when you relocate to another country outside the European Community.

Even though Ireland benefits from being within the privileged categories for entry into the three countries that we've discussed, the paperwork to be waded through and the requirements to be met can be daunting.

Once again, preparation is paramount when making your decision to relocate abroad as even one mistake could prove very inconvenient to you and your family.

If you do make the transition successfully, you will encounter a whole new world of experience and opportunity.

FURTHER READING AND INFORMATION

Australia

Department of Foreign Affairs and Trade, Australia: www. dfat.gov.au/sydney/index.html

Visas for Australia Company, 'Australian Visa Agents': www. visasforaustralia.co.uk

Canada

Department of Citizenship and Immigration Canada, 'Visiting Canada: Temporary Resident Visas': www.cic.gc.ca/english/visit/apply-how.asp

For Canadian visas, see: www.migrationabroad.com/en/canada_visas.asp

United Arab Emirates

'Dubai: Visa Requirements and Visas': www.propdubai.com/articles/21/index.php

General

Irish Abroad, 'Visa Information Ireland': <u>www.irishabroad.com/travel/info-ireland/visa-ireland.aspx</u>

For overseas construction jobs, see: <u>www.constructionjobs.ie</u>

9

Managing Stress and Positive Thinking

Jane McNicholas

Being made redundant is a very stressful experience. Challenges might include facing the unknown, making decisions, applying for jobs, attending interviews and planning further education or a new business venture. All this at a time when you may be feeling angry or apprehensive, and are perhaps finding it hard to focus or motivate yourself. Add to this the pressures of family and finance and your stress levels may feel out of control. Successfully managing your stress becomes an important factor that can help you negotiate this transitionary phase. Having an understanding of what stress is can help in the subsequent management of it.

Stress is a natural feature of everyday life. It is not necessarily damaging; indeed, it may be advantageous in that it can prompt a heightened performance and lead to healthy adaptation. Damaging effects on your health, well-being, performance, productivity and relationships occur when you are exposed to prolonged, persistent or critically high levels of stress.

175

Definition

There are so many definitions of stress, ranging from those that are based on what stress *does* to us to those definitions that highlight the *relationship* between us and what is making us stressed. The following definitions give some idea of how people have struggled with defining stress.

'Stress is a reality – like love or electricity – unmistakable in experience, yet difficult to define.'
                    (E. Kennedy, *On Becoming a Counsellor*, 1977)

'Stress is the...non-specific response of the body to demands made on it.'
                    (H. Selye, *Stress Without Distress*, 1974)

'Stress is a particular relationship between the person and the environment that is appraised by the person as taxing or exceeding his or her resources and endangering his or her well-being.'
    (R.S. Lazarus and S. Folkman, *Stress, Appraisal and Coping*, 1984)

'Some definitions of stress are so broad that they include essentially anything that might happen to someone.'
    (G.R. Elliot and C. Eisdorfer (eds), *Stress and Human Health*, 1982)

So if we struggle to say what stress is, how do we begin to tackle what it does?
Several approaches can be taken:

1. We can look at all the things that make us stressed (stressors)
2. We can look at our responses: the physical, behavioural, cognitive and emotional reactions we experience when we are stressed

3. We can look at what coping strategies we have and what new ones we might need to develop.

These three categories are returned to later in this chapter when we look at how we can manage stress.

Symptoms of Stress

When faced with a threat, the body's defences set off an automatic response known as 'fight-or-flight'. The specific signs and symptoms of stress vary widely from person to person. Having an understanding of why our bodies react the way they do can be useful both in reassuring us that our response is 'normal', and to aid in recognising our early warning signs so that we can take preventative action.

The fight-or-flight response can take many forms, all of which are designed to prepare a person for emergency action. From an evolutionary perspective, this response kept humans alive: cavemen and cavewomen needed to react (and quickly) to stress. Picture the situation of caveman walking through the forest one morning and meeting a ferocious lion. He wouldn't be doing himself any favours by simply standing there.

The stress response immediately affects the heart, lungs and circulation: the heart rate and blood pressure increase instantaneously; breathing becomes rapid, and the lungs take in more oxygen – useful if you have to run. The spleen discharges red and white blood cells, allowing the blood to transport more oxygen throughout the body. Blood flow may actually increase by 300–400 per cent, priming the muscles, lungs and brain for added demands. Heart rate and blood flow to the large muscles increase so we can run faster and fight harder – all useful when faced with a lion.

Blood vessels under the skin constrict to prevent blood loss in case of injury. The stress effect moves blood flow away from the skin to support the heart and muscle tissues. The physical effect is cool, clammy and sweaty skin. The scalp also tightens so that the hair seems to stand up.

Pupils dilate so we can see better, and our blood sugar level increases, giving us an energy boost and speeding up the reaction time. At the same time, body processes, not essential to immediate survival, are suppressed. Fluids are diverted from nonessential locations, including the mouth. This causes dryness and difficulty in talking. (It would not be essential to talk to the lion.) In addition, stress can cause spasms of the throat muscles, making it difficult to swallow. The digestive and reproductive systems slow down, growth hormones are switched off and the immune response is inhibited.

A part of the brain called the hypothalamus sets off a chemical alarm. The sympathetic nervous system responds by releasing a flood of stress hormones, including adrenaline, norepinephrine and cortisol. Cortisol is important in organising systems and organs throughout the body (including the heart, lungs, circulation, metabolism, immune system and skin) to deal quickly with danger. Neurotransmitters (chemical messengers) called catecholamines, particularly dopamine, norepinephrine, and epinephrine (also called adrenaline) activate an area inside the brain called the amygdala, which triggers an emotional response to a stressful event – this emotion is most likely fear. During the stressful event, catecholamines also suppress activity in areas at the front of the brain concerned with short-term memory, concentration, inhibition and rational thought.

The biological stress response is meant to protect and support us. Whilst we might not be faced with many lions nowadays, we have to deal with things that present a threat to our sense of well-being. Additionally, it does not make any difference if it is a real threat or a perceived threat. Just as our ancestors did, we need this response to kick in equally if we actually see a lion or if we just hear an unexpected rustle in the undergrowth that *might* indicate a lion.

Chronic Stress

The problem with the stress response is that the more it's activated, the harder it is to shut off. Instead of levelling off once the crisis has passed, stress hormones, heart rate and blood pressure remain elevated. Extended or repeated activation of the stress response takes a heavy toll on the body. Complications occur if stress becomes persistent because this causes all parts of the body's stress apparatus (the brain, heart, lungs, vessels and muscles) to become chronically over- or under-activated.

Immune System

Chronic stress affects the immune system. It can lower the immune system's response to infections, and may even impair a person's response to immunisations.

Digestive System

The brain and intestines are strongly related and are controlled by many of the same hormones and parts of the nervous system. Prolonged stress can disrupt the digestive system, irritating the large intestine and causing diarrhoea, constipation, cramping and bloating. Irritable bowel syndrome, peptic ulcers and inflammatory bowel disease (Crohn's disease or ulcerative colitis) have all been associated with stress.

Heart

There is thought to be a connection between mental stress and heart disease. Stress activates the part of the nervous system that influences the activities of many organs, including the heart. This could theoretically affect the heart badly:

- Sudden stress increases the pumping action and rate of the heart, while at the same time causing the arteries to constrict (narrow). This restricts blood flow to the heart
- Stress causes blood to become stickier (possibly in preparation for potential injury), increasing the likelihood of an artery-clogging blood clot
- Stress appears to impair the clearance of fat molecules in the body, raising blood-cholesterol levels, at least temporarily
- Chronic stress may lead to the production of immune factors called cytokines. Cytokines produce a damaging inflammatory response, which is now believed to be responsible for damage to the arteries. Such damage contributes to heart disease.

Weight and Eating Problems

Stress can have varying effects on eating problems and weight:

- Weight gain: often stress is related to weight gain and obesity. Many people develop cravings for salt, fat and sugar to counteract tension and, therefore, gain weight. If you are stressed, weight gain can occur even with a healthy diet, however. In addition, the weight gained is often abdominal fat, a predictor of diabetes and heart problems

- Weight loss: some people suffer a loss of appetite and lose weight during periods of stress. In rare cases, stress may trigger hyperactivity of the thyroid gland, stimulating appetite but causing the body to burn up calories at a faster rate than normal.

Diabetes

Chronic stress has been associated with the development of insulin resistance, a condition in which the body is unable to use insulin effectively to regulate glucose (blood sugar). Insulin resistance is a primary factor in diabetes. Stress can also exacerbate existing diabetes by impairing the patient's ability to manage the disease effectively.

Headaches

Tension-type headache episodes are associated with stress and stressful events. Sometimes the headache doesn't even start until long after a stressful event is over.

Sleep Disturbances

The tensions of unresolved stress frequently cause insomnia, generally keeping the stressed person awake or causing them to wake in the middle of the night or early morning.

Other Disorders

Stress has been related to skin allergies, skin disorders and even hair loss (Alopecia areata). Alopecia areata is hair loss that occurs in localised (individual) patches. Stress is also implicated in increasing the risk of periodontal disease, which is disease of the gums that can cause tooth loss.

As well as the physical or health effects described above, stress affects people's cognitive, emotional and behavioural patterns – how they think, how they feel, and what they do. These are described in more detail later in this chapter.

While unchecked stress is undeniably damaging, there are many things a person can do to control it and reduce its effects. These strategies generally fall into the following categories:

1. Prevention – avoiding stress
2. Managing stress – altering responses to stress
3. Coping with stress – palliative responses to stress.

1. Preventing Stress

Preventing stress is not usually a realistic goal, nor is it totally advisable. There are certain aspects of a stress response that can increase our motivation and ability to change and respond. The term for this positive stress is 'eustress'. The negative aspect of stress is 'distress'. It is interesting that we generally just throw it all together and term the lot 'stress'.

We might be able to avoid certain amounts of stress, but if we make this our focus then it seems that we might be following a path of passivity. For example, there can be little doubt for most people that personal relationships are a cause of stress. They are a cause of much joy, fulfilment and excitement as well. If we were to try to avoid stress then an argument could be made that we would be better off not risking getting involved in a relationship because there is no guarantee that we would not at some time in the future be stressed as a result. We might be better off not venturing out in the car because there might be traffic chaos. In fact, we might be better off not going out of the house at all because there are bound to be things out there that are stressful.

2. Managing Stress

Stress management involves the following factors:

- Recognising the symptoms of stress
- Identifying the causes
- Taking action to address the causes, thereby reducing the symptoms.

Recognising the Symptoms

Symptoms may be biological, cognitive, emotional or behavioural. Stress is commonly viewed as an emotional response to not being able to cope, so 'admitting' to feeling stressed is often regarded as a personal failure.
Cognitive symptoms can include:

- Memory problems
- Indecisiveness
- Inability to concentrate
- Trouble thinking clearly
- Poor judgment
- Seeing only the negative side of things
- Anxious or racing thoughts
- Constant worrying

- Loss of objectivity
- Fearful anticipation.

Emotional symptoms can include:

- Moodiness
- Agitation
- Restlessness
- Shortness of temper
- Irritability
- Impatience
- Inability to relax
- Feeling tense and 'on edge'
- Feeling overwhelmed
- Sense of loneliness and isolation
- Depression or general unhappiness.

Behavioural symptoms can include:

- Eating more or less
- Sleeping too much or too little
- Isolating yourself from others
- Procrastination
- Neglecting responsibilities
- Using alcohol, cigarettes or drugs to relax
- Nervous habits (e.g. nail biting, pacing)
- Teeth grinding or jaw clenching
- Overdoing activities (e.g. exercising, shopping)
- Overreacting to unexpected problems.

Identifying the Causes

The pressures and demands that cause stress are known as stressors. Stressors are usually considered as being negative, such as an exhausting work schedule. However, anything that forces a person to adjust can be a stressor. This includes positive events such as getting married or receiving a promotion. Regardless of whether an event is good or bad, if it requires an adjustment that strains coping skills and adaptive resources, the end result is stress. Causes of stress vary from person to person, time to time, context to context. To one person a dripping tap could be a source of intense irritation and stress, to another the dripping could be a pleasant rhythmic sound! The important factor is that we start to become aware of what it is that we find difficult, and what we struggle to cope with.

In a 1967 article in the *Journal of Psychosomatic Research*, T.S. Holmes and R.H. Rahe outlined an inventory that describes the top ten stressful life events:

1. Spouse's death
2. Divorce
3. Marriage separation
4. Jail term
5. Death of a close relative
6. Injury or illness
7. Marriage
8. Job loss
9. Marriage reconciliation
10. Retirement.

Daily causes of stress include: environmental stressors such as an unsafe neighbourhood, pollution, noise and uncomfortable living conditions; family and relationship stressors; social stressors such as poverty, financial pressures, racial and sexual discrimination or harassment, unemployment, isolation and a lack of social support.

Additionally, internal causes can generate stress. Perfectionism, low self-esteem, excessive or unexpressed anger and unrealistic expectations or beliefs can all contribute to a person's stress levels.

Taking Action – Managing Your Thinking

'[Coping processes are] *the person's cognitive and behavioural efforts to manage (reduce, minimise, master or tolerate) the internal and external demands of the person–environment transaction that is appraised as taxing or exceeding the resources of the person.'*
  (Folkman *et al.*, 'Dynamics of a Stressful Encounter', 1986)

'There is nothing about the environmental event on its own or about the person in isolation from the environmental context that makes an event stressful.'
  (D. Bartlett, *Stress: Perspectives and Processes*, 1998)

Stress comes from the interaction and discrepancy between the person and his or her environment. As the environment and individual present too many variables to control or plan for, then *how* this interaction is dealt with becomes the critical issue. This suggests that the individual takes the leading role in responding to stress. Whether that is by a physical, cognitive or emotional strategy, the important factor is that it is a response rather than a reaction.

A large part of being able to manage stress is to recognise and manage how you think. When we are stressed, the way we think often becomes, at best, distorted and, at worst, destructive.

The trick to developing more effective coping strategies is first to recognise (as quickly as possible) when you think in self-defeating ways. Only then can you try to stop this type of thinking and replace it with more constructive strategies. One of the central messages of cognitive behavioural therapy is that the thoughts and beliefs we hold have a huge effect on the way we interpret the world and thus how we deal with it. Distorted thinking can prevent us from making accurate assessments and decisions, and at times of stress, such as threatened or actual redundancy, we need to be making clear decisions.

There are several patterns of thinking in response to stress that you may find recognisable.

'All-or-Nothing' Thinking

All-or-nothing thinking or black-and-white thinking is extreme thinking that can lead to extreme emotions and behaviours.

'A' is trying to monitor his diet, eat healthily and lose weight. In a moment of weakness he eats a bar of chocolate. He concludes that his plan is in ruins – what is the point in trying anymore since he can't even stick to a simple diet? This thinking leads to a further two bars of chocolate and a bag of crisps.

Alternatively he could acknowledge that the bar of chocolate was a mistake, be realistic that perhaps inevitably he will make mistakes and return to the plan. In other words he could develop 'both-and' thinking: he is not a success or a failure; he can be ultimately successful in his diet and give in to temptation occasionally.

'Filtered' Thinking

Filtered thinking refers to a bias in how we might process information. We only acknowledge something if it fits in with a belief we hold.

'B' does not have a great view of himself. He notices all the mistakes he makes and even if somebody says 'Well done' and praises him, he discounts this and says something on the lines of, 'She was only trying to make me feel better' or 'She probably felt sorry for me – that's why she said that.' As a result, he feels bad whether he makes a mistake or whether he does well.

On the other hand, 'B' might need to practise acknowledging both positive and negative points – about himself, about others and about the world. One way of doing this might be to push himself to think of something positive every time he thinks of something negative – to 'balance the books'. He could learn to accept compliments more easily – perhaps simply by saying 'Thank you' and not pushing them away.

'Over-Generalisation' Thinking

Over-generalising is when we come to conclusions based on only a small number of events or evidence. It can typically be spotted by the use of words such as 'never' or 'always', as in 'People are always out for what they can get' or 'Nothing ever goes right for me.'

'C' is under pressure financially and finds herself shouting angrily at her child who has just asked for a new game. She concludes that she is always angry with him, that she is a terrible mother and will never be able to get it right.

She could look at the situation from a wider perspective and ask herself whether she really is a terrible mother for shouting. Does this one incident cancel out all the good, caring things she does for her child? If shouting at the child leads to the conclusion that she is a bad parent, this logic would mean that simply singing a lullaby to the child makes her a great parent – and this

clearly doesn't work. Gaining a perspective that both acknowl-
edges shouting as not ideal and leads to thinking about how she
might deal more effectively with these situations would more
likely resolve the problem.

'Mind-Reading' Thinking

Mind-reading thinking is when we predict the future, most commonly in a negative way. It often prevents us from taking action, leaving us passive and stuck in the same spot.

'D' is feeling down because of work pressures and financial strain. Someone invites him to a match, but he decides that if he goes he will not have a good time; in fact he will more than likely bring everybody else down. So he decides to stay at home.

Another option for 'D' would be to risk going and test whether he would enjoy himself or not.

'Emotional Reasoning' Thinking

When we are stressed we often experience more intense emotions. If we rely on these emotions as indicators of reality then we may end up with a distorted view of reality. We can further compound this possibility because, when we are convinced something is a reality, we stop looking for and don't see any of the evidence that might contradict our views.

'E' is stressed about her work situation – the increased pressure and the air of uncertainty. Her partner is spending longer and longer at his work and coming home later. 'E' feels hurt and angry and concludes that he is obviously having an affair.

Alternatively, she could ask herself what evidence other than her feelings supports her conclusion; might there be another explanation for him working longer hours? Could it be that her feelings are the result of her stress? Would she feel differently if she was not stressed?

'Personalisation' Thinking

This type of thinking occurs when we relate events to ourselves and overlook all other factors that might be involved. It can cause us to feel hurt easily and to feel guilty.

'F' saw that his colleague was upset. His thinking went along the lines of 'What have I done to upset him? I should try to make him feel better.' 'F' was anxious and guilty.

However, 'F' could consider that there are many other things going on in his colleague's life, and chances are that these other things have caused his upset.

'Labelling' Thinking

Labels, and labelling people and events can leave us stuck with a viewpoint that doesn't leave much, if any, room for change and improvement.

'G' has always labelled people on the dole as 'wasters'. He now faces redundancy himself and some of his feelings of desperation focus on how he will be 'no better than the rest of them'. He too will be a 'waster'.

On the other hand, 'G' could start to challenge his label 'waster'. The reasons why people are on the dole are numerous and complex. Reviewing our beliefs and assumptions can allow us to think more flexibly, and perhaps let us see others and ourselves in more than one-dimensional ways.

'Should' Thinking

When we are stressed one of the most noticeable things that happens is that our thinking becomes more rigid. Our thoughts become littered with words such as 'should', 'must', 'have to', 'ought to', 'got to'. This inflexibility might be seen as a direct response to the stress and the need to feel that we are still in control, but it generally leads to a difficulty in adapting rather than increased control.

'H' believes that you should never let anybody down. When he is made redundant, he struggles for a long time. He keeps returning to the line 'But they shouldn't have done that.' This is starting to hamper him looking ahead.

However, 'H' could start to replace the words 'should', 'must', 'have to', ought to' and 'got to' with 'I would like'. In other words, 'I would like people not to let others down.' With this comes an understanding that, while you might have a rule or value that works for you, others may not give it the same priority.

3. Coping with Stress

Palliative Strategies

Even with stress management and prevention, stress is still an everyday fact and its symptoms are experienced on a regular basis. It is therefore important to develop strategies to cope with stress when it does arise. The concepts of exercise, relaxation and paying attention to diet are generally well understood and accepted by most people as a means of reducing stress, and will be discussed below.

The emotional impact of stress also needs to be addressed. In the case of a person being made redundant or facing the prospect of redundancy, the most prominent emotion is often a sense of loss. Losing your job leads to many other losses such as loss of income, status, routine, identity, predictability, security, safety, an imagined future, a lifestyle, self-esteem. Other emotions may include anger and fear.

The most effective strategy to deal with emotions is to express them. This might be to family or friends, or, in a more structured approach, to a counsellor or psychotherapist. Many workplaces have employee assistance programmes (EAPs) in place whereby employees have access to counselling. At times of financial uncertainty, this might make counselling a more viable option.

Relaxation Techniques

Relaxation is a purposeful activity and practice. It is not the practice of collapsing on the sofa when you get home – this is more probably a response to exhaustion! It may seem strange that we need to learn or relearn how to relax. Our thoughts are often so overpowering, especially at times of increased stress, that it is often surprisingly difficult for us to learn how to make time for ourselves. If you doubt this, just try bringing your attention to your breathing and notice how quickly your mind will try to wander or drift off. It might drift into the future or start thinking about things that have happened. These thoughts can be like incessant chatter going on in the background and can drain a lot of our energy. Just letting go of them takes practice.

There are many different approaches to relaxation. A brief outline of the most basic approaches – breathing and muscle relaxation techniques – are presented. The 'further reading' list at the end of this chapter includes some in-depth books on the subject.

Breathing

From the moment we are born to the moment we die, we breathe. We have little conscious control over our breathing. We can hold our breath for a short while or change how deeply or quickly we breathe. Generally we don't pay much attention to it. Relaxation through breathing involves paying attention to our breathing. We can observe it through our nostrils, our chest or our stomach. Feeling the air as it flows in and out is the first step. You don't have to push or force it in or out harder or faster, just feel the rhythm of it. You don't particularly have to think about it, your breath will continue to do its job just as it has for a long time. The trick is just to feel it and be aware of the sensations. Most advice would suggest you focus on your stomach, partly because this is likely to bring you the most peace. Diaphragmatic breathing is when we can relax the muscles of the stomach. Then, as the breath comes in, it can be a little bit longer, the lungs can fill with a little bit more air, and so breathing tends to be slower and deeper. When we are under stress our breathing is often the first thing to be affected. It tends to become shallower and we may experience some discomfort as we find it difficult to take full deep breaths into our lungs. Whilst paying attention to breathing may seem simplistic, it is a powerful tool that can bring a sense of calm almost instantly.

Muscle Relaxation

This technique helps to identify and reduce tension in our bodies. Again, it is very simple. It is often referred to as the body scan because it involves systematically paying attention to our bodies. It may help to lie down on your back to do this.

Close your eyes. Starting with your toes and moving up your body, ask yourself, 'Where am I tense?' Whenever you discover a tense area of your body, focus in on it and exaggerate it slightly so you can become fully aware of it. When you are aware of the muscles in your body that are tense, say to yourself: 'I am tensing my neck muscles [for example] ... I am hurting myself ... I am creating tension in my body.' All muscular tension is self-produced.

Physical Exercise

Physical exercise, and thus physical fitness, has been shown to be strongly correlated to good mental awareness and absence of tension. Walking is probably the best form of exercise. It is flexible (you can do it pretty much anywhere) and it doesn't cost money. Activities that also provide a social, interactive dimension may have a greater impact in managing stress. We give ourselves many reasons for not exercising and the reasons are powerful: 'I'm too tired', 'I don't have enough time', 'I'm too out of shape', 'The weather is bad', 'I'm too embarrassed in front of others', 'It's boring.' Facing up to these excuses is essential, and often involves a fundamental change in your approach to what it means to value yourself and your life.

Nutrition

Nutrition can play an important role in stress management. When a person is under increased stress, their need for all nutrients – especially calcium and the B Vitamins – increases. Supplements or more fresh fruit and vegetables can address this. Stimulants, such as caffeine, which is not only found in coffee but in many types of tea, chocolate, cocoa and cola, actually induce the flight and fight response in our bodies and so can keep us in a perpetual state of tension. Times of stress might be the very times we feel like comfort eating. Our bodies generally have lower levels of energy and so our tendency might be to go for the high sugar or salt foods, but these will actually be counter-productive to our well-being. Focussing on healthy nutrition and diet can help us increase energy levels.

FURTHER READING AND INFORMATION

General

Bartlett, D. (1998), *Stress: Perspectives and Processes*, Buckingham: Open University Press.

Elliot, G.R. and Eisdorfer, C. (eds) (1982), *Stress and Human Health: Analysis and Implications of Research*, a study by the Institute of Medicine/National Academy of Sciences, New York: Springer.

Holmes, T.S. and Rahe, R.H. (1967), 'The Social Readjustment Rating Scale', *Journal of Psychosomatic Research*, vol. 11, no. 2, 213–218.

Kennedy, E. (1977), *On Becoming a Counsellor*, Dublin: Gill & Macmillan.

Lazarus, R.S. and Folkman, S. (1984), *Stress, Appraisal and Coping*, New York: Springer.

Marinoff, Lou (2003), *The Big Questions: How Philosophy Can Change Your Life*, London: Bloomsbury Publishing.

Selye, H. (1974), *Stress Without Distress*, Scarborough: Signet.

Relaxation Techniques

Burns, D.D. (1989), *The Feeling Good Handbook*, New York: William Morrow and Company, Inc.

Davidson, J.(1999), *The Complete Idiot's Guide to Managing Stress*, US: Alpha Books.

Davis, M. and Eshelman, E.R. (2000), *The Relaxation and Stress Reduction Workbook*, Oakland, CA: New Harbinger Publications.

Folkman, S. and Lazarus, R.S. *et al.* (1986), 'Dynamics of a Stressful Encounter: Cognitive Appraisal, Coping, and Encounter Outcomes', *Journal of Personality and Social Psychology*, vol. 50, no. 5, 992–1003.

Kabat-Zinn, Jon (1996), *Full Catastrophe Living: How to Cope with Stress, Pain and Illness Using Mindfulness Meditation*, London: Piatkus Books.

10

Turning Redundancy into Advantage

Tom McGuinness

Throughout this book, the emphasis has been on treating redundancy as a life experience that can be turned into an advantage. This is easier for some than for others. Realising that you are not alone and that help is there, if you know where and how to look for it, is important.

Overcoming the initial shock of redundancy, gathering all your facts and setting goals early on will give you the clarity and confidence to look ahead positively. Taking one step at a time and considering all your options will be far better in the medium term than rushing around without any sense of direction. Assessing your situation realistically but constructively will give you a sound basis for moving forward. Remember to seek help and, if you conclude that you have a professional weakness in a particular area, it may be far better to address it at this stage than to ignore it. You now have the opportunity to do this.

In the previous chapter, we discussed in depth the impact of stress and how the way we think is so important in determining how successful we are. Redundancy forces us into change and this means new ways of thinking. Bringing about new ways of thinking does not happen on its own. We must actually do something different to create a new beginning. To do this, most of us need a structured approach to succeed and the following constitute the main elements of an effective structured personal change programme. This consists of four phases:

1. Preparing for change
2. Developing support
3. Managing the transition
4. Maintaining and building momentum.

Phase 1: Preparing for Change

Phase 1 is about setting objectives that are realistic but challenging. These may relate to going after new job opportunities, setting up a business or going back to further education.

We need to know exactly what we want to achieve before we set about taking action. A good way of doing this is to think up various scenarios. From these scenarios, select the one that is most likely to lead to the achievement of the outcomes you want and which scenario would require the easiest means to get where you want to be. We do this naturally in most circumstances but writing down the various scenarios adds more structure and allows us to revisit them later on and adapt them to suit our needs as we progress.

Getting ready for change is about getting into the right frame of mind and setting about creating the right environment. 'Psyching' yourself up broadly describes what is necessary. Setting down a future point in time when you will start and getting mentally prepared is key to a successful launch of a personal change initiative. Collecting evidence of why change is necessary to bolster your resolve is important at this early stage. You need as many reasons as possible to move forward. This awareness will come about in many ways, such as internal reflection, exposure to new situations and experiences, feedback from peers and colleagues, and generally by seeking information related to what you want to achieve. We also need to develop our commitment to letting go of certain things that would inhibit achieving our goals. These may be long-established habits and will not be easily shed.

By putting a goal in place, you will become automatically more conscious of matters that relate to it. When we buy a new car we begin to notice how many models of the same kind are on the road. Our brain, because it has to contend with so much information, automatically blocks out irrelevant information. It only takes on board what we are focussed upon and what is needed to protect ourselves from harm. The minute we set a goal, we facilitate information about that goal to come into our conscious mind.

List out the key benefits of the change and use this list as a support throughout the period of change.

Phase 2: Developing Support

Phase 1 of the exercise is extremely positive and to most people enjoyable. We can use all our creativity and imagination. But there are barriers that must be overcome. These might be within us and may be of a psychological and emotional nature. Previous experience and conditioning may be holding us back. It is wise to surface these feelings early and gain as much understanding as possible of their nature and how they will impact on you as you move forward. Being prepared to face up to those 'moments of truth' will be a deciding factor in whether you continue or give up.

Of course, the barriers may be material or physical in nature. Financial concerns, access to supports and other considerations may be handicaps to progress. Being aware of these barriers and building contingency plans will enable you to overcome them or else focus the change programme in a different direction. If the change is significant in nature, it is unlikely that you will be able to accomplish it on your own without external supports and help. Get a counsellor or a friend or family member on board early on and involve them in your change initiative. One of the most important ways to bring about change is to alter your context or environment. For instance, if you want to lose weight then you will have to alter your dining and snacking patterns as well as what you eat. Remember, if you keep doing the same thing, you will keep getting the same result.

Remaining in the old environment will make change difficult. Altering your environment as much as possible will allow you to put new habits in place and, more importantly, sustain them.

Phase 3: Managing the Transition

Managing the transition to achieve your goals requires careful planning and sustainability of effort. There will be times when you falter and your plan should take this into account. Setting out the various actions required and the milestones along the way enables you to break down the change into manageable bites or stages. Each milestone should be seen as an accomplishment in itself and used as a reason to continue on the journey. Timetabling your actions will give you a clear picture of what will emerge as you progress. Having this clear picture in your mind and a sense of how you will feel at each stage provides positive motivation along the way. Enlist the supports that you identified in Phase 2. Sometimes you will find that some of your concerns will not materialise as you had thought. At other times, there will be unexpected barriers that you had not foreseen. See these as part of the learning process and face up to them. Build new supports and actions to overcome them.

By continuing towards your goal, you will be surprised at your success. Continually using each success to build your confidence frequently results in the 'snowball' effect. Thus, as you progress, the task becomes easier and the overall likelihood of achieving your goal greater.

Phase 4: Sustaining Momentum

It is relatively easy to think up a goal and set about achieving it – it is only when the journey commences that the commitment is tested. This is why so many diets do not succeed. Sustaining momentum is critical. What can you do to ensure that this is done? First, by undertaking the three previous phases you will be in a position to take what comes and deal positively with difficulties as they arise. Second, by creating a strong reward and reinforcement system you will sustain your progress. These rewards should be as concrete as possible, such as having a night out at an event you particularly like or putting money saved in a transparent container so that you can see it grow. However, rewards should also be emotional, in the form of, for example, positive feedback from a friend or someone you respect.

More often, this feedback should come from your own personal reflection and meditation, and your use of self-talk will be critical to this process. Ensuring your self-talk is constructive and positive is probably the most important way you can ensure that your momentum is sustained. Remember to be patient. Persistence is what will pay dividends. Recognise that it is a journey and that completing the journey will have worthwhile benefits.

Depending on what level of change is required, the above structure can be adjusted to suit your needs. If the change is small, it is still worthwhile planning it, but obviously with less rigour than where the change is much bigger, such as returning to education or changing career. Remember also that many small changes can lead to a large change. So taking small steps could be best for you. However, having a long-range view keeps all your efforts focussed and will likely lead to greater success.

Keeping Active in Your Search

If it takes you a while to find a new position, there are a number of things that will increase your chances of success and keep you sane. Keep active. Isolating yourself at home is absolutely the wrong thing to do. You may not have much money but there are always positive ways of spending and investing your time. Join the local drama group or choir. Continue to meet with friends even if it is just to go for a walk. Consider volunteer work or undertake short training courses – anything that keeps you thinking and talking to people.

Many people who have been made redundant have discovered the seeds of a satisfying new career in the activities they took on to keep themselves busy while they looked for work. Based on your skills alone, getting the right opportunity won't be easy at present. Networking and being available is a very good way to open doors and generate new career prospects. Some useful tips are:

- Keep in touch: maintain your existing contacts and attempt to grow your network. Talk regularly to ex-colleagues and other people who may able to funnel news of opportunities in your direction, but not in such a way that they will start to feel used! Email selected people whom you know may be able to influence getting you a position – even a temporary one
- In a recession, employers are still recruiting. Often they don't advertise for fear of being inundated with applications. Up to 90 per cent of positions are said to be in the 'hidden' job market – filled without ever being advertised. This is why networking is so important. It is good to attend events and to join a local business or voluntary organisation. If you are member of a professional body, attend at least some of their events and promote your availability through them. Keeping yourself out there will ensure you are making contacts, gathering information about prospects and, perhaps even more importantly, keeping up morale by doing something positive
- The Internet is constantly providing new ways of communicating and networking. Remember, the first accomplishment is getting yourself noticed. Perhaps you should create your own website on Twitter (www.twitter.com). Put up your CV and a blog tracking

your quest. There are networking websites such as LinkedIn (www.linkedIn.com) where you can build a virtual network online. This puts you in contact with others who may be requiring someone like you or a service you can provide

- To increase your chances of getting a job sometimes you must build a relationship. In building a relationship, being able to give something to a prospective employer is important. If you are targeting a particular employer then maybe you can provide information on the competition, knowledge of a particular expertise or technology that would be beneficial – something that would give their business a leg up. Initially, they may not be willing to pay you but if you appear useful, energetic and of value, then they may see it as worthwhile offering you a position. See Talent Tank (www.talenttank.ie), a website where individuals offer their experience to employers free of charge for an initial short duration. This allows an individual to get experience in a new industry and to keep his or her CV alive, while showing their talents to a potential employer – with no cost to the employer

- Keep your supporters around you. Do not be too proud or ashamed to ask for help from other people. Have people on hand who can build your confidence or get you out of the doldrums. Make sure you think about what you can do for them in return. On the opposite side, try not to spend too much time with people who have a negative outlook. There is a danger that they can infect you with similar emotions

- Keep innovating. If the methods of job hunting that you have used in the past do not seem to be working,

try something different. If your existing contacts are not forthcoming, try making new contacts
- Coming up with new ideas is not always easy, but good career coaching can often help you to take a different perspective on your situation. There are plenty of career coaches available but make sure that the one you choose has a proven track record
- One of the great problems will be fear of change and of taking on new challenges. While there are no easy ways to get over these fears, they must be confronted, understood and overcome. As outlined above, thinking creatively and in a structured way about strategies to do this and enlisting the support of your family and friends will be helpful. Professional help is also available. Many people are shy of seeking such support but the returns can be enormous. Going it alone may be considered brave, but getting help will increase your chances of success.

Learning from the Redundancy Experience

You will learn much from each part of the redundancy experience – about yourself and about how you react in certain situations. You will have to develop new coping mechanisms and new ways of dealing with change. This will stand you in good stead as you progress. Remember the lessons from the experience and take time out to consider your career options in the future. Build on opportunities for development and growth. Take advantage of opportunities for training and development. Nurture your career so that you maximise your potential and achieve maximum personal satisfaction from your work life.

At different stages of life, new priorities emerge. Many find it hard to leave behind existing habits and practices and alter their priorities. However, modern work life is forever changing and old guarantees are disappearing. This demands that we adapt to the new environment. Outside events, such as redundancy, can be triggers for such change. However, real change comes from within us, not just from external events. Taking control of your life and the changes that you need to make is the best guarantee of realising your goals and becoming fulfilled as a human being.

Further Reading and Information

Bate, N. (2009), *Beat the Recession: A Blueprint for Business Survival*, UK: Infinite Ideas.

Harrold, F. (2001), *Be Your Own life Coach: How to Take Control of Your Life and Achieve Your Wildest Dreams*, UK: Coronet Books.

McGuinness, T. (2004), *From Redundancy to Success: Powerful Ways of Forging a New Career after Redundancy*, Dublin: Blackhall Publishing.

Index

Index

Index

Index

Index

Index